I0236670

A LITTLE REBEL

A NOVEL

THE DUCHESS

(Margaret Wolfe Hungerford)

1st WORLD
LIBRARY
Literary Society

A Little Rebel

Margaret Wolfe Hungerford

© 1st World Library, 2006
PO Box 2211
Fairfield, IA 52556
www.1stworldlibrary.com
First Edition

LCCN: 2006935246

Softcover ISBN: 1-4218-2498-1
Hardcover ISBN: 1-4218-2398-5
eBook ISBN: 1-4218-2598-8

Purchase *"A Little Rebel"*
as a traditional bound book at:
www.1stWorldLibrary.com/purchase.asp?ISBN=1-4218-2498-1

1st World Library is a literary, educational organization
dedicated to:

- Creating a free internet library of downloadable ebooks

- Hosting writing competitions and offering book
publishing scholarships.

Interested in more 1st World Library books?
contact: literacy@1stworldlibrary.com
Check us out at: www.1stworldlibrary.com

1st World Library Literary Society

Giving Back to the World

"If you want to work on the core problem, it's early school literacy."

- James Barksdale, former CEO of Netscape

"No skill is more crucial to the future of a child, or to a democratic and prosperous society, than literacy."

- Los Angeles Times

Literacy... means far more than learning how to read and write... The aim is to transmit... knowledge and promote social participation."

- UNESCO

"Literacy is not a luxury, it is a right and a responsibility. If our world is to meet the challenges of the twenty-first century we must harness the energy and creativity of all our citizens."

- President Bill Clinton

"Parents should be encouraged to read to their children, and teachers should be equipped with all available techniques for teaching literacy, so the varying needs and capacities of individual kids can be taken into account."

- Hugh Mackay

CHAPTER I

"Perplex'd in the extreme."

"The memory of past favors is like a rainbow, bright, vivid and beautiful."

The professor, sitting before his untasted breakfast, is looking thevery picture of dismay. Two letters lie before him; one is in his hand, the other is on the table-cloth. Both are open; but of one, the opening lines - that tell of the death of his old friend - are all he has read; whereas he has read the other from start to finish, already three times. It is from the old friend himself, written a week before his death, and very urgent and very pleading. The professor has mastered its contents with ever-increasing consternation.

Indeed so great a revolution has it created in his mind, that his face - (the index of that excellent part of him) - has, for the moment, undergone a complete change. Any ordinary acquaintance now entering the professor's rooms (and those acquaintances might be whittled down to quite a *little* few), would hardly have known him. For the abstraction that, as a rule, characterizes his features - the way he has of looking at you, as if he doesn't see you, that harasses the simple, and enrages the others - is all gone! Not a trace of it remains. It has given place to terror, open and unrestrained.

"A girl!" murmurs he in a feeble tone, falling back in his chair.

And then again, in a louder tone of dismay - "A *girl!*" He pauses again, and now again gives way to the fear that is destroying him - "A *grown* girl!"

After this, he seems too overcome to continue his reflections, so goes back to the fatal letter. Every now and then, a groan escapes him, mingled with mournful remarks, and extracts from the sheet in his hand -

"Poor old Wynter! Gone at last!" staring at the shaking signature at the end of the letter that speaks so plainly of the coming icy clutch that should prevent the poor hand from forming ever again even such sadly erratic characters as these. "At least," glancing at the half-read letter on the cloth - "*this* tells me so. His solicitor's, I suppose. Though what Wynter could want with a solicitor - Poor old fellow! He was often very good to me in the old days. I don't believe I should have done even as much as I *have* done, without him.... It must be fully ten years since he threw up his work here and went to Australia! ... ten years. The girl must have been born before he went," - glances at letter - "'My child, my beloved Perpetua, the one thing on earth I love, will be left entirely alone. Her mother died nine years ago. She is only seventeen, and the world lies before her, and never a soul in it to care how it goes with her. I entrust her to you - (a groan). To you I give her. Knowing that if you are living, dear fellow, you will not desert me in my great need, but will do what you can for my little one.'"

"But what is that?" demands the professor, distractedly. He pushes his spectacles up to the top of his head, and then drags them down again, and casts them wildly into the sugar-bowl. "What on earth am I to do with a girl of seventeen? If it had been a boy! even *that* would have been bad enough - but a girl! And, of course - I know Wynter - he has died without a penny. He was bound to do that, as he always lived without one. *Poor old Wynter!*" - as if a little ashamed of himself. "I don't see how I can afford to put her out to nurse." He pulls himself up with a start. "To nurse! a girl of seventeen! She'll want to be

Margaret Wolfe Hungerford

going out to balls and things - at her age."

As if smitten to the earth by this last awful idea, he picks his glasses out of the sugar and goes back to the letter.

"You will find her the dearest girl. Most loving, and tender-hearted; and full of life and spirits."

"Good heavens!" says the professor. He puts down the letter again, and begins to pace the room. "'Life and spirits.' A sort of young kangaroo, no doubt. What will the landlady say? I shall leave these rooms" - with a fond and lingering gaze round the dingy old apartment that hasn't an article in it worth ten sous - "and take a small house - somewhere - and ... But - er - - It won't be respectable, I think. I - I've heard things said about - er - things like that. It's no good in *looking* an old fogey, if you aren't one; it's no earthly use" - standing before a glass and ruefully examining his countenance - "in looking fifty if you are only thirty-four. It will be a scandal," says the professor mournfully. "They'll *cut* her, and they'll cut me, and - what the *deuce* did Wynter mean by leaving me his daughter? A real live girl of seventeen! It'll be the death of me," says the professor, mopping his brow. "What" - wrathfully - "that determined spendthrift meant, by flinging his family on *my* shoulders, I - Oh! *Poor* old Wynter!"

Here he grows remorseful again. Abuse a man dead and gone, and one, too, who had been good to him in many ways when he, the professor, was younger than he is now, and had just quarrelled with a father who was always only too prone to quarrel with anyone who gave him the chance seems but a poor thing. The professor's quarrel with his father had been caused by the young man's refusal to accept a Government appointment - obtained with some difficulty - for the very insufficient and, as it seemed to his father, iniquitous reason, that he had made up his mind to devote his life to science. Wynter, too, was a scientist of no mean order, and would, probably, have made his mark in the world, if the world and its pleasures had not made their mark on him. He had been young Curzon's coach at one time, and finding the lad a kindred spirit, had opened out to him his own large store of knowledge, and steeped him in that great sea of which no man yet has drank enough - for all begin, and leave it, athirst.

Poor Wynter! The professor, turning in his stride up and down the narrow, uncomfortable room, one of the many that lie off the Strand, finds his eyes resting on that other letter - carelessly opened, barely begun.

From Wynter's solicitor! It seems ridiculous that Wynter should have *had* a solicitor. With a sigh, he takes it up, opens it out and begins to read it. At the end of the second page, he starts, re-reads a sentence or two, and suddenly his face becomes illuminated. He throws up his head. He cackles a bit. He looks as if he wants to say something very badly - "Hurrah," probably - only he has forgotten how to do it, and finally goes back to the letter again, and this time - the third time - finishes it.

Yes. It is all right! Why on earth hadn't he read it *first?* So, the girl is to be sent to live with her aunt after all - an old lady - maiden lady. Evidently living somewhere in Bloomsbury. Miss Jane Majendie. Mother's sister evidently. Wynter's sisters would never have been old maids if they had resembled him, which probably they did - if he had any. What a handsome fellow he was! and such a good-natured fellow too.

The professor colors here in his queer sensitive way, and pushes his spectacles up and down his nose, in another nervous fashion of his. After all, it was only this minute he had been accusing old Wynter of anything but good nature. Well! He had wronged him there. He glances at the letter again.

He has only been appointed her guardian, it seems. Guardian of her fortune, rather than of her.

The old aunt will have the charge of her body, the - er - pleasure of her society - *he*, of the estate only.

Fancy Wynter, of all men, dying rich - actually *rich*. The professor pulls his beard, and involuntarily glances round the somewhat meagre apartment, that not all his learning, not all his success in the scientific world - and it has been not unnoteworthy, so far - has enabled him to improve upon. It has helped him to live, no doubt, and distinctly outside the line of *want*, a thing to be grateful for, as his family having in a measure abandoned him, he, on his part, had abandoned his family in a *measure* also (and with reservations), and it would have been impossible to him, of all men, to confess himself beaten, and return to them for assistance of any kind. He could never have enacted the part of the prodigal son. He knew this in earlier days, when husks were for the most part all he had to sustain him. But the mind requires not even the material husk, it lives on better food than that, and in his case mind had triumphed over body, and borne it triumphantly to a safe, if not as yet to a victorious, goal.

Yet Wynter, the spendthrift, the erstwhile master of him who now could be *his* master, has died, leaving behind him a fortune. What was the sum? He glances back to the sheet in his hand and verifies his thought. Yes - eighty thousand pounds! A good fortune even in these luxurious days. He has died worth L80,000, of which his daughter is sole heiress!

Before the professor's eyes rises a vision of old Wynter. They used to call him "old," those boys who attended his classes, though he was as light-hearted as the best of them, and as handsome as a dissipated Apollo. They had all loved him, if they had not revered him, and, indeed, he had been generally regarded as a sort of living and lasting joke amongst them.

Curzon, holding the letter in his hand, and bringing back to his memory the handsome face and devil-may-care expression of his tutor, remembers how the joke had widened, and reached its height when, at forty years of age, old Wynter had flung up his classes, leaving them all *plante la* as it were, and declared his intention of starting life anew and making a pile for himself in some new world.

Well! it had not been such a joke after all, if they had only known. Wynter *had* made that mythical "pile," and had left his daughter an heiress!

Not only an heiress, but a gift to Miss Jane Majendie, of somewhere in Bloomsbury.

The professor's disturbed face grows calm again. It even occurs to him that he has not eaten his breakfast. He so *often* remembers this, that it does not trouble him. To pore over his books (that are overflowing every table and chair in the uncomfortable room) until his eggs are India-rubber, and his rashers gutta-percha, is not a fresh experience. But though this morning both eggs and rasher have attained a high place in the leather department, he enters on his sorry repast with a glad heart.

Sweet are the rebounds from jeopardy to joy! And he has so *much* of joy! Not only has he been able to shake from his shoulders that awful incubus - and ever-present ward - but he can be sure that the absent ward is so well-off with regard to this word's goods, that he need never give her so much as a passing thought - dragged, *torn* as that thought would be from his beloved studies.

The aunt, of course, will see about her fortune. *He* has has only a perfunctory duty - to see that the fortune is not squandered. But he is safe there. Maiden ladies *never* squander! And the girl, being only seventeen, can't possibly squander it herself for some time.

Perhaps he ought to call on her, however. Yes, of course, he must call. It is the usual thing to call on one's ward. It will be a terrible business no doubt. *All* girls belong to the genus nuisance. And *this* girl will be at the head of her class no doubt. "Lively, spirited," so far went the parent. A regular hoyden may be read between those kind parental lines.

The poor professor feels hot again with nervous agitation as he imagines an interview between him and the wild, laughing, noisy, perhaps horsey (they all ride in Australia) young woman to whom he is bound to make his bow.

How soon must this unpleasant interview take place? Once more he looks back to the solicitor's letter. Ah! On Jan. 3rd her father, poor old Wynter, had died, and on the 26th of May, she is to be "on view" at Bloomsbury! and it is now the 2nd of February. A respite! Perhaps, who knows? She may never arrive at Bloomsbury at all! There are young men in Australia, a hoyden, as far as the professor has read (and that is saying a good deal), would just suit the man in the bush.

CHAPTER II

"A maid so sweet that her mere sight made glad men
sorrowing."

Nevertheless the man in the bush doesn't get her.

Time has run on a little bit since the professor suffered many
agonies on a certain raw February morning, and now it is the
30th of May, and a glorious finish too to that sweet month.

Even into this dingy old room, where at a dingy old table the
professor sits buried in piles of notes, and with sheets of
manuscript knee-deep scattered around him, the warm glad
sun is stealing; here and there, the little rays are darting,
lighting up a dusty corner here, a hidden heap of books there.
It is, as yet, early in the afternoon, and the riotous beams, who
are no respecter of persons, and who honor the righteous and
the ungodly alike, are playing merrily in this sombre chamber,
given so entirely up to science and its prosy ways, daring even
now to dance lightly on the professor's head, which has begun
to grow a little bald.

"The golden sun, in splendor likest heav'n,"

is proving perhaps a little too much for the tired brain in the
small room. Either that, or the incessant noises in the street
outside, which have now been enriched by the strains of a
broken-down street piano, causes him to lay aside his pen and

Margaret Wolfe Hungerford

lean back in a weary attitude in his chair.

What a day it is! How warm! An hour ago he had delivered a brilliant lecture on the everlasting Mammoth (a fresh specimen just arrived from Siberia), and is now paying the penalty of greatness. He had done well - he knew that - he had been *interesting*, that surest road to public favor - he had been applauded to the echo; and now, worn out, tired in mind and body, he is living over again his honest joy in his success.

In this life, however, it is not given us to be happy for long. A knock at the professor's door brings him back to the present, and the knowledge that the landlady - a stout, somewhat erratic person of fifty - is standing on his threshold, a letter in her hand.

"For you, me dear," says she, very kindly, handing the letter to the professor.

She is perhaps the one person of his acquaintance who has been able to see through the professor's gravity and find him *young*.

"Thank you," says he. He takes the letter indifferently, opens it languidly, and - Well, there isn't much languor after the perusal of it.

The professor sits up; literally this time slang is unknown to him; and re-reads it. *That girl has come!* There can't be any doubt of it. He had almost forgotten her existence during these past tranquil months, when no word or hint about her reached him, but now, *here* she is at last, descending upon him like a whirlwind.

A line in a stiff, uncompromising hand apprises the professor of the unwelcome fact. The "line" is signed by "Jane Majendie," therefore there can be no doubt of the genuineness of the news contained in it. Yes! that girl *has* come!

The professor never swears, or he might now perhaps have given way to reprehensible words.

Instead of that, he pulls himself together, and determines on immediate action. To call upon this ward of his is a thing that must be done sooner or later, then why not sooner? Why not at once? The more unpleasant the duty, the more necessity to get it off one's mind without delay.

He pulls the bell. The landlady appears again.

"I must go out," says the professor, staring a little helplessly at her.

"An' a good thing too," says she. "A saint's day ye might call it, wid the sun. An' where to, sir, dear? Not to thim rascally sthudents, I do thrust?"

"No, Mrs. Mulcahy. I - I am going to see a young lady," says the professor simply.

"The divil!" says Mrs. Mulcahy with a beaming smile. "Faix, that's a turn the right way anyhow. But have ye thought o' yer clothes, me dear?"

"Clothes?" repeats the professor vaguely.

"Arrah, wait," says she, and runs away lightly, in spite of her fifty years and her too, too solid flesh, and presently returns with the professor's best coat and a clothes brush that, from its appearance, might reasonably be supposed to have been left behind by Noah when he stepped out of the Ark. With this latter (having put the coat on him) she proceeds to belabor the professor with great spirit, and presently sends him forth shining - if not *in*ternally, at all events *ex*ternally.

In truth the professor's mood is not a happy one. Sitting in the hansom

Margaret Wolfe Hungerford

that is taking him all too swiftly to his destination, he dwells with terror on the girl - the undesired ward - who has been thrust upon him. He has quite made up his mind about her. An Australian girl! One knows what to expect *there*! Health unlimited; strength tremendous; and noise - *much* noise.

Yes, she is sure to be a *big* girl. A girl with branching limbs, and a laugh you could hear a mile off. A young woman with no sense of the fitness of things, and a settled conviction that nothing could shake, that "'Strailia" is *the* finest country on earth! A bouncing creature who *never* sits down; to whom rest or calm is unknown, and whose highest ambition will be to see the Tower and the wax-works.

Her hair is sure to be untidy; hanging probably in straight, black locks over her forehead, and her frock will look as if it had been pitchforked on to her, and requires only the insubordination of *one* pin to leave her without it again.

The professor is looking pale, but has on him all the air of one prepared for *anything* as the maid shows him into the drawing-room of the house where Miss Jane Majendie lives.

His thoughts are still full of her niece. *Her* niece, poor woman, and *his* ward - poor *man*! when the door opens and *some one* comes in.

Some one!

The professor gets slowly on to his feet, and stares at the advancing apparition. Is it child or woman, this fair vision? A hard question to answer! It is quite easy to read, however, that "some one" is very lovely!

"It is you; Mr. Curzon, is it not?" says the vision.

Her voice is sweet and clear, a little petulant perhaps, but still *very* sweet. She is quite small - a *little* girl - and clad in deep mourning. There is something pathetic about the dense black surrounding such a radiant face, and such a childish figure. Her eyes are fixed on the professor, and there is evident anxiety in their hazel depths; her soft lips are parted; she seems hesitating as if not knowing whether she shall smile or sigh. She has raised both her hands as if unconsciously, and is holding them clasped against her breast. The pretty fingers are covered with costly rings. Altogether she makes a picture - this little girl, with her brilliant eyes, and mutinous mouth, and soft black clinging gown. Dainty-sweet she looks,

"Sweet as is the bramble-flower."

"Yes," says the professor, in a hesitating way, as if by no means certain of the fact. He is so vague about it, indeed, that "some one's" dark eyes take a mischievous gleam.

"Are you *sure?*" says she, and looks up at him suddenly, a little sideways perhaps, as if half frightened, and gives way to a naughty sort of little laugh. It rings through the room, this laugh, and has the effect of frightening her *altogether* this time. She checks herself, and looks first down at the carpet with the big roses on it, where one little foot is wriggling in a rather nervous way, and then up again at the professor, as if to see if he is thinking bad things of her. She sighs softly.

"Have you come to see me or Aunt Jane?" asks she; "because Aunt Jane is out - *I'm glad to say*" - this last pianissimo.

"To see you," says the professor absently. He is thinking! He has taken her hand, and held it, and dropped it again, all in a state of high bewilderment.

Is *this* the big, strong, noisy girl of his imaginings? The bouncing creature with untidy hair, and her clothes pitch-forked on to her?

"Well - I hoped so," says she, a little wistfully as it seems to him, every trace of late sauciness now gone, and with it the sudden shyness. After many days the professor grows

16   Margaret Wolfe Hungerford

accustomed to these sudden transitions that are so puzzling yet so enchanting, these rapid, inconsequent, but always lovely changes

"From grave to gay, from lively to severe."

"Won't you sit down?" says his small hostess gently, touching a chair near her with her slim fingers.

"Thank you," says the professor, and then stops short.

"You are -"

"Your ward," says she, ever so gently still, yet emphatically. It is plain that she is now on her very *best* behavior. She smiles up at him in a very encouraging way. "And you are my guardian, aren't you?"

"Yes," says the professor, without enthusiasm. He has seated himself, not on the chair she has pointed out to him, but on a very distant lounge. He is conscious of a feeling of growing terror. This lovely child has created it, yet why, or how? Was ever guardian mastered by a ward before? A desire to escape is filling him, but he has got to do his duty to his dead friend, and this is part of it.

He has retired to the far-off lounge with a view to doing it as distantly as possible, but even this poor subterfuge fails him. Miss Wynter, picking up a milking-stool, advances leisurely towards him, and seating herself upon it just in front of him, crosses her hands over her knees and looks expectantly up at him with a charming smile.

"*Now* we can have a good talk," says she.

CHAPTER III

"And if you dreamed how a friend's smile
And nearness soothe a heart that's sore,
You might be moved to stay awhile
Before my door."

"About?" begins the professor, and stammers, and ceases.

"Everything," says she, with a little nod. "It is impossible to talk to Aunt Jane. She doesn't talk, she only argues, and always wrongly. But you are different. I can see that. Now tell me," - she leans even more forward and looks intently at the professor, her pretty brows wrinkled as if with extreme and troublous thought - "What are the duties of a guardian?"

"Eh?" says the professor. He moves his glasses up to his forehead and then pulls them down again. Did ever anxious student ask him question so difficult of answer as this one - that this small maiden has propounded?

"You can think it over," says she most graciously. "There is no hurry, and I am quite aware that one isn't made a guardian *every* day. Do you think you could make it out whilst I count forty?"

"I think I could make it out more quickly if you didn't count at all," says the professor, who is growing warm. "The duties of a guardian - are - er - to - er - to see that one's ward is

Margaret Wolfe Hungerford

comfortable and happy."

"Then there is a great deal of duty for *you* to do," says she solemnly, letting her chin slip into the hollow of her hand.

"I know - I'm sure of it," says the professor with a sigh that might be called a groan. "But your aunt, Miss Majendie - your mother's sister - can -"

"I don't believe she's my mother's sister," says Miss Wynter calmly. "I have seen my mother's picture. It is lovely! Aunt Jane was a changeling - I'm sure of it. But never mind her. You were going to say -?"

"That Miss Majendie, who is virtually your guardian - can explain it all to you much better than I can."

"Aunt Jane is *not* my guardian!" The mild look of enquiry changes to one of light anger. The white brow contracts. "And certainly she could never make one happy and comfortable. Well - what else?"

"She will look after -"

"I told you I don't care about Aunt Jane. Tell me what you can do -"

"See that your fortune is not -"

"I don't care about my fortune either," with a little gesture. "But I *do* care about my happiness. Will you see to *that?*"

"Of course," says the professor gravely.

"Then you will take me away from Aunt Jane!" The small vivacious face is now all aglow. "I am not happy with Aunt Jane. I" - clasping her hands, and letting a quick, vindictive fire light her eyes - "I *hate* Aunt Jane. She says things about poor papa that - *Oh!* how I hate her!"

"But - you shouldn't - you really should not. I feel certain you ought not," says the professor, growing vaguer every moment.

"Ought I not?" with a quick little laugh that is all anger and no mirth. "I *do* though, for all that! I" - pausing, and regarding him with a somewhat tragic air that sits most funnily upon her - "am not going to stay here much longer!"

"*What?*" says the professor aghast. "But my dear - Miss Wynter, I'm afraid you *must.*"

"Why? What is she to me?"

"Your aunt."

"That's nothing - nothing at all - even a *guardian* is better than that. And you are my guardian. Why," coming closer to him and pressing five soft little fingers in an almost feverish fashion upon his arm, "why can't *you* take me away?"

"*I!*"

"Yes, yes, you." She comes even nearer to him, and the pressure of the small fingers grows more eager - there is something in them now that might well be termed coaxing. "*Do,*" says she.

"Oh! Impossible!" says the professor. The color mounts to his brow. He almost *shakes* off the little clinging fingers in his astonishment and agitation. Has she no common-sense - no knowledge of the things that be?

She has drawn back from him and is regarding him somewhat strangely.

"Impossible to leave Aunt Jane?" questions she. It is evident she has not altogether understood, and yet is feeling puzzled. "Well," defiantly, "we shall see!"

Margaret Wolfe Hungerford

"*Why* don't you like your Aunt Jane?" asks the professor distractedly. He doesn't feel nearly as fond of his dead friend as he did an hour ago.

"Because," lucidly, "she *is* Aunt Jane. If she were *your* Aunt Jane you would know."

"But my dear -"

"I really wish," interrupts Miss Wynter petulantly, "you wouldn't call me 'my dear.' Aunt Jane calls me that when she is going to say something horrid to me. Papa -" she pauses suddenly, and tears rush to her dark eyes.

"Yes. What of your father?" asks the professor hurriedly, the tears raising terror in his soul.

"You knew him - speak to me of him," says she, a little tremulously.

"I knew him well indeed. He was very good to me, when - when I was younger. I was very fond of him."

"He was good to everyone," says Miss Wynter, staring hard at the professor. It is occurring to her that this grave sedate man with his glasses could never have been younger. He must always have been older than the gay, handsome, *debonnaire* father, who had been so dear to her.

"What are you going to tell me about him?" asks the professor gently.

"Only what he used to call me - *Doatie*! I suppose," wistfully, "you couldn't call me that?"

"I am afraid not," says the professor, coloring even deeper.

"I'm sorry," says she, her young mouth taking a sorrowful curve. "But don't call me Miss Wynter, at all events, or 'my dear.' I do so want someone to call me by my Christian name," says the poor child sadly.

"Perpetua - is it not?" says the professor, ever so kindly.

"No - 'Pet,'" corrects she. "It's shorter, you know, and far easier to say."

"Oh!" says the professor. To him it seems very difficult to say. Is it possible she is going to ask him to call her by that familiar - almost affectionate - name? The girl must be mad.

"Yes - much easier," says Perpetua; "you will find that out, after a bit, when you have got used to calling me by it. Are you going now, Mr. Curzon? Going *so soon*?"

"I have classes," says the professor.

"Students?" says she. "You teach them? I wish I was a student. I shouldn't have been given over to Aunt Jane then, or," with a rather wilful laugh, "if I had been I should have led her, oh!" rapturously, "*such a life!*"

It suggests itself to the professor that she is quite capable of doing that now, though she is *not* of the sex male.

"Good-bye," says he, holding out his hand.

"You will come soon again?" demands she, laying her own in it.

"Next week - perhaps."

"Not till then? I shall be dead then," says she, with a rather mirthless laugh this time. "Do you know that you and Aunt Jane are the only two people in all London whom I know?"

"That is terrible," says he, quite sincerely.

"Yes. Isn't it?"

"But soon you will know people. Your aunt has acquaintances. They - surely they will call; they will see you - they -"

"Will take an overwhelming fancy to me? just as you have done," says she, with a quick, rather curious light in her eyes, and a tilting of her pretty chin. "There! *go*," says she, "I have some work to do; and you have your classes. It would never do for you to miss *them*. And as for next week! - make it next month! I wouldn't for the world be a trouble to you in any way."

"I shall come next week," says the professor, troubled in somewise by the meaning in her eyes. What is it? Simple loneliness, or misery downright? How young she looks - what a child! That tragic air does not belong to her of right. She should be all laughter, and lightness, and mirth -

"As you will," says she; her tone has grown almost haughty; there is a sense of remorse in his breast as he goes down the stairs. Has he been kind to old Wynter's child? Has he been true to his trust? There had been an expression that might almost be termed despair in the young face as he left her. Her face, with that expression on it, haunts him all down the road.

Yes. He will call next week. What day is this? Friday. And Friday next he is bound to deliver a lecture somewhere - he is not sure where, but certainly somewhere. Well, Saturday then he might call. But that -

Why not call Thursday - or even Wednesday?

Wednesday let it be. He needn't call every week, but he had said something about calling next week, and - she wouldn't care, of course - but one should keep their word. What a strange little face she has - and strange manners, and - not able to get on evidently with her present surroundings.

What an old devil that aunt must be.

CHAPTER IV

"Dear, if you knew what tears they shed,
Who live apart from home and friend,
To pass my house, by pity led,
Your steps would tend."

He makes the acquaintance of the latter very shortly. But requires no spoon to sup with her, as Miss Majendie's invitations to supper, or indeed to luncheon, breakfast or dinner, are so few and rare that it might be rash for a hungry man to count on them.

The professor, who has felt it to be his duty to call on his ward regularly every week, has learned to know and (I regret to say) to loathe that estimable spinster christened Jane Majendie.

After every visit to her house he has sworn to himself that "*this one*" shall be his last, and every Wednesday following he has gone again. Indeed, to-day being Wednesday in the heart of June, he may be seen sitting bolt upright in a hansom on his way to the unlovely house that holds Miss Jane Majendie.

As he enters the dismal drawing-room, where he finds Miss Majendie and her niece, it becomes plain, even to his inexperienced brain, that there has just been a row on somewhere.

Perpetua is sitting on a distant lounge, her small vivacious face

Margaret Wolfe Hungerford

one thunder-cloud. Miss Majendie, sitting on the hardest chair this hideous room contains, is smiling. A terrible sign. The professor pales before it.

"I am glad to see you, Mr. Curzon," says Miss Majendie, rising and extending a bony hand. "As Perpetua's guardian, you may perhaps have some influence over her. I say 'perhaps' advisedly, as I scarcely dare to hope *anyone* could influence a mind so distorted as hers."

"What is it?" asks the professor nervously - of Perpetua, not of Miss Majendie.

"I'm dull," says Perpetua sullenly.

The professor glances keenly at the girl's downcast face, and then at Miss Majendie. The latter glance is a question.

"You hear her," says Miss Majendie coldly - she draws her shawl round her meagre shoulders, and a breath through her lean nostrils that may be heard. "Perhaps *you* may be able to discover her meaning."

"What is it?" asks the professor, turning to the girl, his tone anxious, uncertain. Young women with "wrongs" are unknown to him, as are all other sorts of young women for the matter of that. And *this* particular young woman looks a little unsafe at the present moment.

"I have told you! I am tired of this life. I am dull - stupid. I want to go out." Her lovely eyes are flashing, her face is white - her lips trembling. "*Take* me out," says she suddenly.

"Perpetua!" exclaims Miss Majendie. "How unmaidenly! How immodest!"

Perpetua looks at her with large, surprised eyes.

"Why?" says she.

"I really think," interrupts the professor hurriedly, who sees breakers ahead, "if I were to take Perpetua for a walk - a drive - to - er - to some place or other - it might destroy this *ennui* of which she complains. If you will allow her to come out with me for an hour or so, I -"

"If you are waiting for *my* sanction, Mr. Curzon, to that extraordinary proposal, you will wait some time," says Miss Majendie slowly, frigidly. She draws the shawl still closer, and sniffs again.

"But -"

"There is no 'But,' sir. The subject doesn't admit of argument. In my young days, and I should think" - scrutinizing him exhaustively through her glasses - "*in yours*, it was not customary for a young *gentlewoman* to go out walking, alone, with '*a man*'!!" If she had said with a famished tiger, she couldn't have thrown more horror into her tone.

The professor had shrunk a little from that classing of her age with his, but has now found matter for hope in it.

"Still - my age - as you suggest - so far exceeds Perpetua's - I am indeed so much older than she is, that I might be allowed to escort her wherever it might please her to go."

"The *real* age of a man now-a-days, sir, is a thing impossible to know," says Miss Majendie. "You wear glasses - a capital disguise! I mean nothing offensive - *so far* - sir, but it behoves me to be careful, and behind those glasses, who can tell what demon lurks? Nay! No offence! An *innocent* man would *feel* no offence!"

"Really, Miss Majendie!" begins the poor professor, who is as red as though he were the guiltiest soul alive.

"Let me proceed, sir. We were talking of the ages of men."

"We?"

"Certainly! It was you who suggested the idea, that, being so much older than my niece, Miss Wynter, you could therefore escort her here and there - in fact *everywhere* - in fact" - with awful meaning - "*any* where!"

"I assure you, madam," begins the professor, springing to his feet - Perpetua puts out a white hand.

"Ah! let her talk," says she. "*Then* you will understand."

"But men's ages, sir, are a snare and a delusion!" continues Miss Majendie, who has mounted her hobby, and will ride it to the death. "Who can tell the age of any man in this degenerate age? We look at their faces, and say *he* must be so and so, and *he* a few years younger, but looks are vain, they tell us nothing. Some look old, because they *are* old, some look old - through *vice!*"

The professor makes an impatient gesture. But Miss Majendie is equal to most things.

"'Who excuses himself *accuses* himself,'" quotes she with terrible readiness. "Why that gesture, Mr. Curzon? I made no mention of *your* name. And, indeed, I trust your age would place you outside of any such suspicion, still, I am bound to be careful where my niece's interests are concerned. You, as her guardian, if a *faithful* guardian" (with open doubt, as to this, expressed in eye and pointed finger), "should be the first to applaud my caution."

"You take an extreme view," begins the professor, a little feebly, perhaps. That eye and that pointed finger have cowed him.

"One's views *have* to be extreme in these days if one would continue in the paths of virtue," said Miss Majendie. "*Your* views," with a piercing and condemnatory glance, "are evidently *not* extreme. One word for all, Mr. Curzon, and this argument is at an end. I shall not permit my niece, with my permission, to walk with you or any other man whilst under my protection."

"I daresay you are right - no doubt - no doubt," mumbles the professor, incoherently, now thoroughly frightened and demoralized. Good heavens! What an awful old woman! And to think that this poor child is under her care. He happens at this moment to look at the poor child, and the scorn *for him* that gleams in her large eyes perfects his rout. To say that she was *right!*

"If Perpetua wishes to go for a walk," says Miss Majendie, breaking through a mist of angry feeling that is only half on the surface, "I am here to accompany her."

"I don't want to go for a walk - with you," says Perpetua, rudely it must be confessed, though her tone is low and studiously reserved. "I don't want to go for a walk *at all.*" She pauses, and her voice chokes a little, and then suddenly she breaks into a small passion of vehemence. "I want to go somewhere, to *see* something," she cries, gazing imploringly at Curzon.

"To *see* something!" says her aunt, "why it was only last Sunday I took you to Westminster Abbey, where you saw the grandest edifice in all the world."

"Most interesting place," says the professor, *sotto voce*, with a wild but mad hope of smoothing matters down for Perpetua's sake.

If it *was* for Perpetua's sake, she proves herself singularly ungrateful. She turns upon him a small vivid face, alight with indignation.

"You support her," cries she. "*You!* Well, I shall tell you! I" - defiantly - "I don't want to go to churches at all. I want to go to *theatres*! There!"

There is an awful silence. Miss Majendie's face is a picture! If the girl had said she wanted to go to the devil instead of to the theatre, she could hardly have looked more horrified. She takes a step forward, closer to Perpetua.

"Go to your room! And pray - *pray* for a purer mind!" says she. "This is hereditary, all this! Only prayer can cast it out. And remember, this is the last word upon this subject. As long as you are under *my* roof you shall never go to a sinful place of amusement. I forbid you ever to speak of theatres again."

"I shall not be forbidden!" says Perpetua. She confronts her aunt with flaming eyes and crimson cheeks. "I *do* want to go to the theatre, and to balls, and dances, and *everything*. I" - passionately, and with a most cruel, despairing longing in her young voice, "want to dance, to laugh, to sing, to amuse myself - to be the gayest thing in all the world!"

She stops as if exhausted, surprised perhaps at her own daring, and there is silence for a moment, a *little* moment, and then Miss Majendie looks at her.

"'The gayest thing in all the world:' *and your father only four months dead*!" says she, slowly, remorselessly.

All in a moment, as it were, the little crimson angry face grows white - white as death itself. The professor, shocked beyond words, stands staring, and marking the sad changes in it. Perpetua is trembling from head to foot. A frightened look has come into her beautiful eyes - her breath comes quickly. She is as a thing at bay - hopeless, horrified. Her lips part as if she would say something. But no words come. She casts one anguished glance at the professor, and rushes from the room.

It was but a momentary glimpse into a heart, but it was terrible. The professor turns upon Miss Majendie in great wrath.

"That was cruel - uncalled for!" says he, a strange feeling in his heart that he has not time to stop and analyze *then*. "How could you hurt her so? Poor child! Poor girl! She *loved* him!"

"Then let her show respect to his memory," says Miss Majendie vindictively. She is unmoved - undaunted.

"She was not wanting in respect." His tone is hurried. This woman with the remorseless eye is too much for the gentle professor. "All she *does* want is change, amusement. She is young. Youth must enjoy."

"In moderation - and in proper ways," says Miss Majendie stonily. "In moderation," she repeats mechanically, almost unconsciously. And then suddenly her wrath gets the better of her, and she breaks out into a violent range. That one should dare to question *her* actions! "Who are *you?*" demands she fiercely, "that you should presume to dictate right and wrong to *me.*"

"I am Miss Wynter's guardian," says the professor, who begins to see visions - and all the lower regions let loose at once. Could an original Fury look more horrible than this old woman, with her grey nodding head, and blind vindictive passion. He hears his voice faltering, and knows that he is edging towards the door. After all, what can the bravest man do with an angry old woman, except to get away from her as quickly as possible? And the professor, though brave enough in the usual ways, is not brave where women are concerned.

"Guardian or no guardian, I will thank you to remember you are in *my* house!" cries Miss Majendie, in a shrill tone that runs through the
professor's head.

"Certainly. Certainly," says he, confusedly, and then he slips out of the room, and having felt the door close behind him, runs tumultuously down the staircase. For years he has not gone down any staircase so swiftly. A vague, if unacknowledged, feeling that he is literally making his escape from a vital danger, is lending wings to his feet. Before him lies the hall-door, and that way safety lies, safety from that old gaunt, irate figure upstairs. He is not allowed to reach, however - just yet.

A door on the right side of the hall is opened cautiously; a shapely little head is as cautiously pushed through it, and two anxious red lips whisper: -

"Mr. Curzon," first, and then, as he turns in answer to the whisper, "Sh - *Sh*!"

CHAPTER V

"My love is like the sea,
As changeful and as free;
Sometimes she's angry, sometimes rough,
Yet oft she's smooth and calm enough -
Ay, much too calm for me."

It is Perpetua. A sad-eyed, a tearful-eyed Perpetua, but a lovely Perpetua for all that.

"Well?" says he.

"*Sh!*" says she again, shaking her head ominously, and putting her forefinger against her lip. "Come in here," says she softly, under her breath.

"Here," when he does come in, is a most untidy place, made up of all things heterogeneous. Now that he is nearer to her, he can see that she has been crying vehemently, and that the tears still stand thick within her eyes.

"I felt I *must* see you," says she, "to tell you - to ask you. To - Oh! you *heard* what she said! Do - do *you* think -?"

"Not at all, not at all," declares the professor hurriedly. "Don't - *don't* cry, Perpetua! Look here," laying his hand nervously upon her shoulder and giving her a little angry shake. "*Don't* cry! Good heavens! Why should you mind that awful old woman?"

Nevertheless, he had minded that awful old woman himself very considerably.

"But - it *is* soon, isn't it?" says she. "I know that myself, and yet -" wistfully - "I can't help it. I *do* want to see things, and to amuse myself."

"Naturally," says the professor.

"And it isn't that I *forget* him," says she in an eager, intense tone, "I *never* forget him - never - never. Only I do want to laugh sometimes and to be happy, and to see Mr. Irving as Charles I."

The climax is irresistible. The professor is unable to suppress a smile.

"I'm afraid, from what I have heard, *that* won't make you laugh," says he.

"It will make me cry then. It is all the same," declares she, impartially. "I shall be enjoying myself, I shall be *seeing* things. You -" doubtfully, and mindful of his last speech - "Haven't you seen him?"

"Not for a long time, I regret to say. I - I'm always so busy," says the professor apologetically.

"*Always* studying?" questions she.

"For the most part," returns the professor, an odd sensation growing within him that he is feeling ashamed of himself.

"'All work and no play,'" begins Perpetua, and stops, and shakes her charming head at him. "*You* will be a dull boy if you don't take care," says she.

A ghost of a little smile warms her sad lips as she says this, and lights up her shining eyes like a ray of sunlight. Then it fades, and she grows sorrowful again.

"Well, *I* can't study," says she.

"Why not?" demands the professor quickly. Here he is on his own ground; and here he has a pupil to his hand - a strange, an enigmatical, but a lovely one. "Believe me knowledge is the one good thing that life contains worth having. Pleasure, riches, rank, *all* sink to insignificance beside it."

"How do you know?" says she. "You haven't tried the others."

"I know it, for all that. I *feel* it. Get knowledge - such knowledge as the short span of life allotted to us will allow you to get. I can lend you some books, easy ones at first, and -"

"I couldn't read *your* books," says she; "and - you haven't any novels, I suppose?"

"No," says he. "But -"

"I don't care for any books but novels," says she, sighing. "Have you read 'Alas?' I never have anything to read here, because Aunt Jane says novels are of the devil, and that if I read them I shall go to hell."

"Nonsense!" said the professor gruffly.

"You mustn't think I'm afraid about *that*" says Perpetua demurely; "I'm not. I know the same place could never contain Aunt Jane and me for long, so *I'm* all right."

The professor struggles with himself for a moment and then gives way to mirth.

"Ah! *now* you are on my side," cries his ward exultantly. She tucks her arm into his. "And as for all that talk about 'knowledge' - don't bother me about that any more. It's a little rude of you, do you know? One would think I was a dunce - that I knew nothing - whereas, I assure you," throwing out her other hand, "I know *quite* as much as most girls, and a great deal more than many. I daresay," putting her head to one side, and examining him thoughtfully, "I know more than you do if it comes to that. I don't believe you know this moment who wrote 'The Master of Ballantrae.' Come now, who was it?"

She leans back from him, gazing at him mischievously, as if anticipating his defeat. As for the professor, he grows red - he draws his brows together. Truly this is a most impertinent pupil! 'The Master of Ballantrae.' It *sounds* like Sir Walter, and yet - The professor hesitates and is lost.

"Scott," says he, with as good an air as he can command.

"Wrong," cries she, clapping her hands softly, noiselessly. "Oh! you *ignorant* man! Go buy that book at once. It will do you more good and teach you a great deal more than any of your musty tomes."

She laughs gaily. It occurs to the professor, in a misty sort of way, that her laugh, at all events, would do *anyone* good.

She has been pulling a ring on and off her finger unconsciously, as if thinking, but now looks up at him.

"If you spoke to her again, when she was in a better temper, don't you think she would let you take me to the theatre some night?" She has come nearer, and has laid a light, appealing little hand upon his arm.

"I am sure it would be useless," says he, taking off his glasses and putting them on again in an anxious fashion. They are both speaking in whispers, and the professor is conscious of feeling a strange sort of pleasure in the thought that he is sharing a secret with her. "Besides," says he, "I couldn't very well come here again."

"Not come again? Why?"

"I'd be afraid," returns he simply. Whereon Miss Wynter, after a second's pause, gives way and laughs "consumedly," as they would have said long, long years before her pretty features saw the light.

"Ah! yes," murmurs she. "How she did frighten you. She brought you to your knees - you actually" - this with keen reproach - "took her part against me."

"I took her part to *help* you;" says the professor, feeling absurdly miserable.

"Yes," sighing, "I daresay. But though I know I should have suffered for it afterwards, it would have done me a world of good to hear somebody tell her his real opinion of her for once. I should like," calmly, "to see her writhe; she makes me writhe very often."

"This is a bad school for you," says the professor hurriedly.

"Yes? Then why don't you take me away from it?"

"If I could - but - Well, I shall see," says he vaguely.

"You will have to be very quick about it," says she. Her tone is quite ordinary; it never suggests itself to the professor that there is meaning beneath it.

"You have *some* friends surely?" says he.

"There is a Mrs. Constans who comes here sometimes to see Aunt Jane. She is a young woman, and her mother was a friend of Aunt Jane's, which accounts for it, I suppose. She seems kind. She said she would take me to a concert soon, but she has not been here for many days, I daresay she has forgotten all about it by this time."

She sighs. The charming face so near the professor's is looking sad again. The white brow is puckered, the soft lips droop. No, she cannot stay *here*, that is certain - and yet it was her father's wish, and who is he, the professor, that he should pretend to know how girls should be treated? What if he should make a mistake? And yet again, should a little brilliant face like that know sadness? It is a problem difficult to solve. All the professor's learning fails him now.

"I hope she will remember. Oh! she *must*," declares he, gazing at Perpetua. "You know I would do what I could for you, but your aunt - you heard her - she would not let you go anywhere with me."

"True," says Perpetua. Here she moves back, and folds her arms stiffly across her bosom, and pokes out her chin, in an aggressive fashion, that creates a likeness on the spot, in spite of the youthful eyes, and brow, and hair. "'Young *gentle*women in *our* time, Mr. Curzon, never, went out walking, *alone*, with *A Man*!'"

The mimicry is perfect. The professor, after a faint struggle with his dignity, joins in her naughty mirth, and both laugh together.

"'*Our*' time! she thinks you are a hundred and fifty!" says Miss Wynter.

"Well, so I am, in a way," returns the professor, somewhat sadly.

"No, you're not," says she. "*I* know better than that. I," patting his arm reassuringly, "can guess your age better than she can. I can see *at once*, that you are not a day older than poor, darling papa. In fact, you may be younger. I am perfectly certain you are not more than fifty."

The professor says nothing. He is staring at her. He is beginning to feel a little forlorn. He has forgotten youth for many days, has youth in revenge forgotten him?

"That is taking off a clear hundred all at once," says she lightly. "No small amount." Here, as if noticing his silence, she looks quickly at him, and perhaps something in his face strikes her, because she goes on hurriedly. "Oh! and what is age after all? I wish *I* were old, and then I should be able to get away from Aunt Jane - without - without any *trouble*."

"I am afraid you are indeed very unhappy here," says the professor gravely.

"I *hate* the place," cries she with a frown. "I shan't be able to stay here. Oh! *why* didn't poor papa send me to live with you?"

Why indeed? That is exactly what the professor finds great difficulty in explaining to her. An "old man" of "fifty" might very easily give a home to a young girl, without comment from the world. But then if an "old man of fifty" *wasn't* an old man of fifty - The professor checks his thoughts, they are growing too mixed.

"We should have been *so* happy," Perpetua is going on, her tone regretful. "We could have gone everywhere together, you and I. I should have taken you to the theatre, to balls, to concerts, to afternoons. You would have been *so* happy, and so should I. You would - wouldn't you?"

The professor nods his head. The awful vista she has opened up to him has completely deprived him of speech.

"Ah! yes," sighs she, taking that deceitful nod in perfect good faith. "And you would have been good to me too, and let me look in at the shop windows. I should have taken such *care* of you, and made your tea for you, just," sadly, "as I used to do for poor papa, and -"

It is becoming too much for the professor.

"It is late. I must go," says he.

*   *   *   *   *

It is a week later when he meets her again. The season is now at its height, and some stray wave of life casting the professor into a fashionable thoroughfare, he there finds he.

Marching along, as usual, with his head in the air, and his thoughts in the ages when dates were unknown, a soft, eager voice calling his name brings him back to the fact that he is walking up Bond Street.

In a carriage, exceedingly well appointed, and with her face wreathed in smiles, and one hand impulsively extended, sits Perpetua. Evidently the owner of the carriage is in the shop making purchases, whilst Perpetua sits without, awaiting her.

"Were you going to cut me?" cries she. "What luck to meet you here. I am having such a *lovely* day. Mrs. Constans has taken me out with her, and I am to dine with her, and go with her to a concert in the evening."

She has poured it all out, all her good news in a breath, as though sure of a sympathetic listener.

He is too good a listener. He is listening so hard, he is looking so intensely, that he forgets to speak, and Perpetua's sudden gaiety forsakes her. Is he angry? Does he think -?

"It's *only* a concert," says she, flushing and hesitating. "Do you think that one should not go to a concert when -"

"Yes?" questions the professor abstractedly, as she comes to a full stop. He has never seen her dressed like this before. She is all in black to be sure, but *such* black, and her air! She looks quite the little heiress, like a little queen indeed - radiant, lovely.

"*Well* - when one is in mourning," says she somewhat impatiently, the color once again dyeing her cheek. Quick tears have sprung to her eyes. They seem to hurt the professor.

"One cannot be in mourning always," says he slowly. His manner is still unfortunate.

"You evade the question," says she frowning. "But a concert *isn't* like a ball, is it?"

"I don't know," says the professor, who indeed has had little knowledge of either for years, and whose unlucky answer arises solely from inability to give her an honest reply.

"You hesitate," says she, "you disapprove then. But," defiantly, "I don't care - a concert is *not* like a ball."

"No - I suppose not!"

"I can see what you are thinking," returns she, struggling with her mortification. "And it is very *hard* of you. Just because *you* don't care to go anywhere, you think *I* oughtn't to care either. That is what is so selfish about people who are old. You," wilfully, "are just as bad as Aunt Jane."

The professor looks at her. His face is perplexed - distressed - and something more, but she cannot read that.

"Well, not quite perhaps," says she, relenting slightly. "But nearly. And if you don't take care you will grow like her. I hate people who lecture me, and besides, I don't see why a guardian should control one's whole life, and thought, and action. A guardian," resentfully, "isn't one's conscience!"

"No. No. Thank Heaven!" says the professor, shocked. Perpetua stares at him a moment and then breaks into a queer little laugh.

"You evidently have no desire to be mixed up with *my*

conscience," says she, a little angry in spite of her mirth. "Well, I don't want you to have anything to do with it. That's *my* affair. But, about this concert," - she leans towards him, resting her hand on the edge of the carriage. "Do you think one should go *nowhere* when wearing black?"

"I think one should do just as one feels," says the professor nervously.

"I wonder if one should *say* just what one feels," says she. She draws back haughtily, then wrath gets the better of dignity, and she breaks out again. "What a *horrid* answer! *You* are unfeeling if you like!"

"*I* am?"

"Yes, yes! You would deny me this small gratification, you would lock me up forever with Aunt Jane, you would debar me from everything! Oh!" her lips trembling, "how I wish - I *wish* - guardians had never been invented."

The professor almost begins to wish the same. Almost - perhaps not quite! That accusation about wishing to keep her locked up forever with Miss Majendie is so manifestly unjust that he takes it hardly. Has he not spent all this past week striving to open a way of escape for her from the home she so detests! But, after all, how could she know that?

"You have misunderstood me," says he calmly, gravely. "Far from wishing you to deny yourself this concert, I am glad - glad from my *heart* - that you are going to it - that some small pleasure has fallen into your life. Your aunt's home is an unhappy one for you, I know, but you should remember that even if - if you have got to stay with her until you become your own mistress, still that will not be forever."

"No, I shall not stay there forever," says she slowly. "And so - you really think -" she is looking very earnestly at him.

"I do, indeed. Go out - go everywhere - enjoy yourself, child, while you can."

He lifts his hat and walks away.

"Who was that, dear?" asks Mrs. Constans, a pretty pale woman, rushing out of the shop and into the carriage.

"My guardian - Mr. Curzon."

"Ah!" glancing carelessly after the professor's retreating figure. "A youngish man?"

"No, old," says Perpetua, "at least I think - do you know," laughing, "when he's *gone* I sometimes think of him as being pretty young, but when he is *with* me, he is old - old and grave!"

"As a guardian should be, with such a pretty ward," says Mrs. Constans, smiling. "His back looks young, however."

"And his laugh *sounds* young."

"Ah! he can laugh then?"

"Very seldom. Too seldom. But when he does, it is a nice laugh. But he wears spectacles, you know - and - well - oh, yes, he *is* old, distinctly old!"

CHAPTER VI

"He is happy whose circumstances suit his temper; but he is more excellent who can suit his temper to any circumstances."

"The idea of *your* having a ward! I could quite as soon imagine your having a wife," says Hardinge. He knocks the ash off his cigar, and after meditating for a moment, leans back in his chair and gives way to irrepressible mirth.

"I don't see why I shouldn't have a wife as well as another," says the professor, idly tapping his forefinger on the table near him. "She would bore me. But a great many fellows are bored."

"You have grasped one great truth if you never grasp another!" says Mr. Hardinge, who has now recovered. "Catch *me* marrying."

"It's unlucky to talk like that," says the professor. "It looks as though your time were near. In Sophocles' time there was a man who -"

"Oh, bother Sophocles, you know I never let you talk anything but wholesome nonsense when I drop in for a smoke with you," says the younger man. "You began very well, with that superstition of yours, but I won't have it spoiled by erudition. Tell me about your ward."

"Would that be nonsense?" says the professor, with a faint smile.

They are sitting in the professor's room with the windows thrown wide open to let in any chance gust of air that Heaven in its mercy may send them. It is night, and very late at night too - the clock indeed is on the stroke of twelve. It seems a long, long time to the professor since the afternoon - the afternoon of this very day - when he had seen Perpetua sitting in that open carriage. He had only been half glad when Harold Hardinge - a young man, and yet, strange to say, his most intimate friend - had dropped in to smoke a pipe with him. Hardinge was fonder of the professor than he knew, and was drawn to him by curious intricate webs. The professor suited him, and he suited the professor, though in truth Hardinge was nothing more than a gay young society man, with just the average amount of brains, but not an ounce beyond that.

A tall, handsome young man, with fair brown hair and hazel eyes, a dark moustache and a happy manner, Mr. Hardinge laughs his way through life, without money, or love, or any other troubles.

"Can you ask?" says he. "Go on, Curzon. What is she like?"

"It wouldn't interest you," says the professor.

"I beg your pardon, it is profoundly interesting; I've got to keep an eye on you, or else in a weak moment you will let her marry you."

The professor moves uneasily.

"May I ask how you knew I *had* a ward?"

"That should go without telling. I arrived here to-night to find you absent and Mrs. Mulcahy in possession, pretending to dust the furniture. She asked me to sit down - I obeyed her.

Margaret Wolfe Hungerford

"'How's the professor?'" said I.

"'Me dear!' said she, 'that's a bad story. He's that distracted over a young lady that his own mother wouldn't know him!'

"I acknowledge I blushed. I went even so far as to make a few pantomimic gestures suggestive of the horror I was experiencing, and finally I covered my face with my handkerchief. I regret to say that Mrs. Mulcahy took my modesty in bad part.

"'Arrah! git out wid ye!' says she, 'ye scamp o' the world. 'Tis a *ward* the masther has taken an' nothin' more.'

"I said I thought it was quite enough, and asked if you had taken it badly, and what the doctor thought of you. But she wouldn't listen to me.

"'Look here, Misther Hardinge,' said she. 'I've come to the conclusion that wards is bad for the professor. I haven't seen the young lady, I confess, but I'm cock-sure that she's got the divil's own temper!'" Hardinge pauses, and turns to the professor - "Has she?" says he.

"N - o," - says the professor - a little frowning lovely crimson face rises before him - and then a laughing one. "No," says he more boldly, "she is a little impulsive, perhaps, but -"

"Just so. Just so," says Mr. Hardinge pleasantly, and then, after a kindly survey of his companion's features, "She is rather a trouble to you, old man, isn't she?"

"She? No," says the professor again, more quickly this time. "It is only this - she doesn't seem to get on with the aunt to whom her poor father sent her - he is dead - and I have to look out for some one else to take care of her, until she comes of age."

"I see. I should think you would have to hurry up a bit," says Mr. Hardinge, taking his cigar from his lips, and letting the smoke curl upwards slowly, thoughtfully. "Impulsive people have a trick of being impatient - of acting for themselves -"

"*She* cannot," says the professor, with anxious haste. "She knows nobody in town."

"Nobody?"

"Except me, and a woman who is a friend of her aunt's. If she were to go to her, she would be taken back again. Perpetua knows that."

"Perpetua! Is that her name? What a peculiar one? Perpetua -"

"Miss Wynter," sharply.

"Perpetua - Miss Wynter! Exactly so! It sounds like - Dorothea - Lady Highflown! Well, *your* Lady Highflown doesn't seem to have many friends here. What a pity you can't send her back to Australia!"

The professor is silent.

"It would suit all sides. I daresay the poor girl is pining for the freedom of her old home. And, I must say, it is hard lines for you. A girl with a temper, to be -"

"I did not say she had a temper."

Hardinge has risen to get himself some whisky and soda, but pauses to pat the professor affectionately on the back.

"Of *course* not! Don't I know you? You would die first! She might worry your life out, and still you would rise up to defend her at every corner. You should get her a satisfactory home as soon as you can - it would ease your mind; and, after all, as she knows no one here, she is bound to behave herself until you can come to her help."

"She would behave herself, as you call it," says the professor angrily, "any and everywhere. She is a lady. She has been well brought up. I am her guardian, she will do nothing without *my* permission!"

"Won't she!"

A sound, outside the door strikes on the ears of both men at this moment. It is a most peculiar sound, as it were the rattle of beads against wood.

"What's that?" said Hardinge. "Everett" (the man in the rooms below,) "is out, I know."

"It's coming here," says the professor.

It is, indeed! The door is opened in a tumultuous fashion, there is a rustle of silken skirts, and there - there, where the gas-light falls full on her from both room and landing - stands Perpetua!

The professor has risen to his feet. His face is deadly white. Mr. Hardinge has risen too.

"Perpetua!" says the professor; it would be impossible to describe his tone.

"I've come!" says Perpetua, advancing into the room. "I have done with Aunt Jane, *for ever*," casting wide her pretty naked arms, "and I have come to you!"

As if in confirmation of this decision, she flings from her on to a distant chair the white opera cloak around her, and stands revealed as charming a thing as ever eye fell upon. She is all in black, but black that sparkles and trembles and shines with every movement. She seems, indeed, to be hung in jet, and out of all this sombre gleaming her white neck rises, pure and fresh and sweet as a little child's. Her long slight arms are devoid of gloves - she had forgotten them, do doubt, but her slender fingers are covered with rings, and round her neck a diamond necklace clings as if in love with its resting place.

Diamonds indeed are everywhere. In her hair, in her breast, on her neck, her fingers. Her father, when luck came to him, had found his greatest joy in decking with these gems the delight of his heart.

The professor turns to Hardinge. That young man, who had risen with the intention of leaving the room on Perpetua's entrance, is now standing staring at her as if bewitched. His expression is half puzzled, half amused. In *this* the professor's troublesome ward? This lovely, graceful -

"Leave us!" says the professor sharply. Hardinge, with a profound bow, quits the room, but not the house. It would be impossible to go without hearing the termination of this exciting episode. Everett's rooms being providentially empty, he steps into them, and, having turned up the gas, drops into a chair and gives way to mirth.

Meantime the professor is staring at Perpetua.

"What has happened?" says he.

Margaret Wolfe Hungerford

CHAPTER VII

"Take it to thy breast;
Though thorns its stem invest,
Gather them, with the rest!"

"She is unbearable. *Unbearable!*" returns Perpetua vehemently. "When I came back from the concert to-night, she - But I won't speak of her. I *won't*. And, at all events, I have done with her; I have left her. I have come" - with decision - "to stay with you!"

"Eh?" says the professor. It is a mere sound, but it expresses a great deal.

"To stay with you. Yes," nodding her head, "it has come to that at last. I warned you it *would*. I couldn't stay with her any longer. I hate her! So I have come to stay with you - *for ever!*"

She has cuddled herself into an armchair, and, indeed, looks as if a life-long residence in this room is the plan she has laid out for herself.

"Great heavens! What do you mean?" asks the poor professor, who should have sworn by the heathen gods, but in a weak moment falls back upon the good old formula. He sinks upon the table next him, and makes ruin of the notes he had been scribbling - the ink is still wet - even whilst Hardinge was with him. Could he only have known it, there are first proofs of them now upon his trousers.

"I have told you," says she. "Good gracious, what a funny room this is! I told you she was abominable to me when I came home to-night. She said dreadful things to me, and I don't care whether she is my aunt or not, I shan't let her scold me for nothing; and - I'm afraid I wasn't nice to her. I'm sorry for that, but - one isn't a bit of stone, you know, and she said something - about my mother," her eyes grow very brilliant here, "and when I walked up to her she apologized for that, but afterwards she said something about poor, *poor* papa - and ... well, that was the end. I told her - amongst *other* things - that I thought she was 'too old to be alive,' and she didn't seem to mind the 'other things' half as much as that, though they were awful. At all events," with a little wave of her hands, "she's lectured me now for good; I shall never see *her* again! I've run away to you! See?"

It must be acknowledged that the professor *doesn't* see. He is still sitting on the edge of the table - dumb.

"Oh! I'm so *glad* I've left her," says Perpetua, with indeed heartfelt delight in look and tone. "But - do you know - I'm hungry. You - you couldn't let me make you a cup of tea, could you? I'm dreadfully thirsty! What's that in your glass?"

"Nothing," says the professor hastily. He removes the half-finished tumbler of whisky and soda, and places it in the open cupboard.

"It looked like *something*," says she. "But what about tea?"

"I'll see what I can do," says he, beginning to busy himself amongst many small contrivances in the same cupboard. It has gone to his heart to hear that she is hungry and thirsty, but even in the midst of his preparations for her comfort, a feeling of rage takes possession of him.

He pulls his head out of the cupboard and turns to her.

"You must be *mad*!" says he.

"Mad? Why?" asks she.

"To come here. Here! And at this hour!"

"There was no other place; and I wasn't going to live under *her* roof another second. I said to myself that she was my aunt, but you were my guardian. Both of you have been told to look after me, and I prefer to be looked after by you. It is so simple," says she, with a suspicion of contempt in her tone, "that I wonder why you wonder at it. As I preferred *you* - of course I have come to live with you."

"You *can't*!" gasps the professor, "you must go back to Miss Majendie at once!"

"To *her*! I'm not going back," steadily. "And even if I would," triumphantly, "I couldn't. As she sleeps at the top of the house (to get *air*, she says), and so does her maid, you might ring until you were black in the face, and she wouldn't hear you."

"Well! you can't stay here!" says the professor, getting off the table and addressing her with a truly noble attempt at sternness.

"Why can't I?" There is some indignation in her tone. "There's lots of room here, isn't there?"

"There is *no* room!" says the professor. This is the literal truth. "The house is full. And - and there are only men here."

"So much the better!" says Perpetua, with a little frown and a great deal of meaning. "I'm tired of women - they're horrid. You're always kind to me - at least," with a glance, "you always used to be, and *you're* a man! Tell one of your servants to make me up a room somewhere."

"There isn't one," says the professor.

"Oh! nonsense," says she leaning back in her chair and yawning softly. "I'm not so big that you can't put me away somewhere. *That woman* says I'm so small that I'll never be a grown-up girl, because I can't grow up any more. Who'd live with a woman like that? And I shall grow more, shan't I?"

"I daresay," says the professor vaguely. "But that is not the question to be considered now. I must beg you to understand, Perpetua, that your staying here is out of the question!"

"Out of the - Oh! I *see*" cries she, springing to her feet and turning a passionately reproachful face on his. "You mean that I shall be in your way here!"

"No, *no*, NO!" cries he, just as impulsively, and decidedly very foolishly; but the sight of her small mortified face has proved too much for him. "Only -"

"Only?" echoes the spoiled child, with a loving smile - the child who has been accustomed to have all things and all people give way to her during her short life. "Only you are afraid *I* shall not be comfortable. But I shall. And I shall be a great comfort to you too - a great *help*. I shall keep everything in order for you. Do you remember the talk we had that last day you came to Aunt Jane's? How I told you of the happy days we should have together, if we *were* together. Well, we are together now, aren't we? And when I'm twenty-one, we'll move into a big, big house, and ask people to dances and dinners and things. In the meantime - " she pauses and glances leisurely around her. The glance is very comprehensive. "To-morrow," says she with decision, "I shall settle this room!"

The professor's breath fails him. He grows pale. To "settle" his room!

"Perpetua!" exclaims he, almost inarticulately, "you don't understand."

"I do indeed," returns she brightly. "I've often settled papa's

Margaret Wolfe Hungerford

den. What! do you think me only a silly useless creature? You shall see! I'll settle *you* too, by and by." She smiles at him gaily, with the most charming innocence, but oh! what awful probabilities lie within her words. *Settle him!*

"Do you know I've heard people talking about you at Mrs. Constans'," says she. She smiles and nods at him. The professor groans. To be talked about! To be discussed! To be held up to vulgar comment! He writhes inwardly. The thought is actual torture to him.

"They said -"

"*What?*" demands the professor, almost fiercely. How dare a feeble feminine audience appreciate or condemn his honest efforts to enlighten his small section of mankind!

"That you ought to be married," says Perpetua, sympathetically. "And they said, too, that they supposed you wouldn't ever be now; but that it was a great pity you hadn't a daughter. *I* think that too. Not about your having a wife. That doesn't matter, but I really think you ought to have a daughter to look after you."

This extremely immoral advice she delivers with a beaming smile.

"*I'll* be your daughter," says she.

The professor goes rigid with horror. What has he *done* that the Fates should so visit him?

"They said something else too," goes on Perpetua, this time rather angrily. "They said you were so clever that you always looked unkempt. That," thoughtfully, "means that you didn't brush your hair enough. Never mind, *I'll* brush it for you."

"Look here!" says the professor furiously, subdued fury no doubt, but very genuine. "You must go, you know. Go, *at once*! D'ye see? You can't stay in this house, d'ye *hear*? I can't permit it. What did your father mean by bringing you up like this!"

"Like what?" She is staring at him. She has leant forward as if surprised - and with a sigh the professor acknowledges the uselessness of a fight between them; right or wrong she is sure to win. He is bound to go to the wall. She is looking not only surprised, but unnerved. This ebullition of wrath on the part of her mild guardian has been a slight shock to her.

"Tell me?" persists she.

"Tell you! what is there to tell you? I should think the veriest infant would have known she oughtn't to come here."

"I should think an infant would know nothing," with dignity. "All your scientific researches have left you, I'm afraid, very ignorant. And I should think that the very first thing even an infant would do, if she could walk, would be to go straight to her guardian when in trouble."

"At this hour?"

"At any hour. What," throwing out her hands expressively, "is a guardian *for*, if it isn't to take care of people?"

The professor gives it up. The heat of battle has overcome him. With a deep breath he drops into a chair, and begins to wonder how long it will be before happy death will overtake him.

But in the meantime, whilst sitting on a milestone of life waiting for that grim friend, what is to be done with her? If - Good heavens! If anyone had seen her come in!

"Who opened the door for you?" demands he abruptly.

"A great big fat woman with a queer voice! Your Mrs. Mulcahy

Margaret Wolfe Hungerford

of course. I remember your telling me about her."

Mrs. Mulcahy undoubtedly. Well, the professor wishes now he had told this ward *more* about her. Mrs. Mulcahy he can trust, but she - awful thought - will she trust him? What is she thinking now?

"I said, 'Is Mr. Curzon at home?' and she said, 'Well I niver!' So I saw she was a kindly, foolish, poor creature with no sense, and I ran past her, and up the stairs, and I looked into one room where there were lights but you weren't there, and then I ran on again until I saw the light under *your* door, and," brightening, "there you were!"

Here *she* is now at all events, at half-past twelve at night!

"Wasn't it fortunate I found you?" says she. She is laughing a little, and looking so content that the professor hasn't the heart to contradict her - though where the fortune comes in -

"I'm starving," says she, gaily, "will that funny little kettle soon boil?" The professor has lit a spirit-lamp with a view to giving her some tea. "I haven't had anything to eat since dinner, and you know she dines at an ungodly hour. Two o'clock! I didn't know I wanted anything to eat until I escaped from her, but now that I have got *you*," triumphantly, "I feel as hungry as ever I can be."

"There is nothing," says the professor, blankly. His heart seems to stop beating. The most hospitable and kindly of men, it is terrible to him to have to say this. Of course Mrs. Mulcahy - who, no doubt, is still in the hall waiting for an explanation, could give him something. But Mrs. Mulcahy can be unpleasant at times, and this is safe to be a "time." Yet without her assistance he can think of no means by which this pretty, slender, troublesome little ward of his can be fed.

"Nothing!" repeats she faintly. "Oh, but surely in that cupboard over there, where you put the glass, there is something; even bread and butter I should like."

She gets up, and makes an impulsive step forward, and in doing so brushes against a small rickety table, that totters feebly for an instant and then comes with a crash to the ground, flinging a whole heap of gruesome dry bones at her very feet.

With a little cry of horror she recoils from them. Perhaps her nerves are more out of order than she knows, perhaps the long fast and long drive here, and her reception from her guardian at the end of it - so different from what she had imagined - have all helped to undo her. Whatever be the cause, she suddenly covers her face with her hands and bursts into tears.

"Take them away!" cries she frantically, and then - sobbing heavily between her broken words - "Oh, I see how it is. You don't want me here at all. You wish I hadn't come. And I have no one but you - and poor papa said you would be good to me. But you are *sorry* he made you my guardian. You would be glad if I were *dead*! When I come to you in my trouble you tell me to go away again, and though I tell you I am hungry, you won't give me even some bread and butter! Oh!" passionately, "if *you* came to *me* starving, I'd give *you* things, but - you -"

"*Stop!*" cries the professor. He uplifts his hands, and, as though in the act of tearing his hair, rushes from the room, and staggers downstairs to those other apartments where Hardinge had elected to sit, and see out the farce, comedy, or tragedy, whichever it may prove, to its bitter end.

The professor bursts in like a maniac!

Margaret Wolfe Hungerford

CHAPTER VIII

"The house of everyone is to him as his castle and fortress, as well for his defence against injury and violence as for his repose."

"She's upstairs still," cries he in a frenzied tone. "She says she has come *for ever*. That she will not go away. She doesn't understand. Great Heaven! What I am to do?"

"She?" says Hardinge, who really in turn grows petrified for the moment - *only* for the moment.

"That girl! My ward! All women are *demons*!" says the professor bitterly, with tragic force. He pauses as if exhausted.

"*Your* demon is a pretty specimen of her kind," says Hardinge, a little frivolously under the circumstances it must be confessed. "Where is she now?"

"Upstairs!" with a groan. "She says she's *hungry*, and I haven't a thing in the house! For goodness sake think of something, Hardinge."

"Mrs. Mulcahy!" suggests Hardinge, in anything but a hopeful tone.

"Yes - ye-es," says the professor. "You - *you* wouldn't ask her for something, would you, Hardinge?"

"Not for a good deal," says Hardinge, promptly. "I say," rising, and going towards Everett's cupboard, "Everett's a Sybarite, you know, of the worst kind - sure to find something here, and we can square it with him afterwards. Beauty in distress, you know, appeals to all hearts. *Here we are!*' holding out at arm's length a pasty. "A 'weal and ammer!' Take it! The guilt be on my head! Bread - butter - pickled onions! Oh, *not* pickled onions, I think. Really, I had no idea even Everett had fallen so low. Cheese! - about to proceed on a walking tour! The young lady wouldn't care for that, thanks. Beer! No. *No.* Sherry-Woine!"

"Give me that pie, and the bread and butter," says the professor, in great wrath. "And let me tell you, Hardinge, that there are occasions when one's high spirits can degenerate into offensiveness and vulgarity!"

He marches out of the room and upstairs, leaving Hardinge, let us hope, a pray to remorse. It is true, at least of that young man, that he covers his face with his hands and sways from side to side, as if overcome by some secret emotion. Grief - no-doubt.

Perpetua is graciously pleased to accept the frugal meal the professor brings her. She even goes so far as to ask him to share it with her - which invitation he declines. He is indeed sick at heart - not for himself - (the professor doesn't often think of himself) - but for her. And where is she to sleep? To turn her out now would be impossible! After all, it was a puerile trifling with the Inevitable, to shirk asking Mrs. Mulcahy for something to eat for his self-imposed guest - because the question of *Bed* still to come! Mrs. Mulcahy, terrible as she undoubtedly can be, is yet the only woman in the house, and it is imperative that Perpetua should be given up to her protection.

Whilst the professor is writhing in spirit over this ungetoutable fact, he becomes aware of a resounding knock at his door. Paralyzed, he gazes in the direction of the sound. It *can't* be

Hardinge, he would never knock like that! The knock in itself, indeed, is of such force and volume as to strike terror into the bravest breast. It is - it *must* be - the Mulcahy!

And Mrs. Mulcahy it is! Without waiting for an answer, that virtuous Irishwoman, clad in righteous indignation and a snuff-colored gown, marches into the room.

"May I ask, Mr. Curzon," says she, with great dignity and more temper, "what may be the meanin' of all this?"

The professor's tongue cleaves to the roof of his mouth, but Perpetua's tongue remains normal. She jumps up, and runs to Mrs. Mulcahy with a beaming face. She has had something to eat, and is once again her own buoyant, wayward, light-hearted little self.

"Oh! it is all right *now*, Mrs. Mulcahy," cries she, whilst the professor grows cold with horror at this audacious advance upon the militant Mulcahy. "But do you know, he said first he hadn't anything to give me, and I was starving. No, you mustn't scold him - he didn't mean anything. I suppose you have heard how unhappy I was with Aunt Jane? - he's told you, I daresay," - with a little flinging of her hand towards the trembling professor - "because I know" - prettily - "he is very fond of you - he often speaks to me about you. Oh! Aunt Jane is *horrid*! I *should* have told you about how it was when I came, but I wanted so much to see my guardian, and tell *him* all about it, that I forgot to be nice to anybody. See?"

There is a little silence. The professor, who is looking as guilty as if the whole ten commandments have been broken by him at once, waits, shivering, for the outburst that is so sure to come.

It doesn't come, however! When the mists clear away a little, he finds that Perpetua has gone over to where Mrs. Mulcahy is standing, and is talking still to that good Irishwoman. It is a whispered talk this time, and the few words of it that he catches go to his very heart.

"I'm afraid he didn't *want* me here," Perpetua is saying, in a low distressed little voice - "I'm sorry I came now - but, you don't *know* how cruel Aunt Jane was to me, Mrs. Mulcahy, you don't indeed! She - she said such unkind things about - about -" Perpetua breaks down again - struggles with herself valiantly, and finally bursts out crying. "I'm tired, I'm sleepy," sobs she miserably.

Need I say what follows? The professor, stung to the quick by those forlorn sobs, lifts his eyes, and - behold! he sees Perpetua gathered to the ample bosom of the formidable, kindly Mulcahy.

"Come wid me, me lamb," says that excellent woman. "Bad scran to the one that made yer purty heart sore. Lave her to me now, Misther Curzon, dear, an' I'll take a mother's care of her." (This in an aside to the astounded professor.) "There now, alanna! Take courage now! Sure 'tis to the right shop ye've come, anyway, for 'tis daughthers I have meself, me dear - fine, sthrappin' girls as could put you in their pockits. Ye poor little crather! Oh! Murther! Who could harm the likes of ye? Faix, I hope that ould divil of an aunt o' yours won't darken these doors, or she'll git what she won't like from Biddy Mulcahy. There now! There now! 'Tis into yer bed I'll tuck ye meself, for 'tis worn-out ye are - God help ye!"

She is gone, taking Perpetua with her. The professor rubs his eyes, and then suddenly an overwhelming sense of gratitude towards Mrs. Mulcahy takes possession of him. *What* a woman! He had never thought so much moral support could be got out of a landlady - but Mrs. Mulcahy has certainly tided him safely over *one* of his difficulties. Still, those that remain are formidable enough to quell any foolish present attempts at relief of mind. "To-morrow, and to-morrow, and to-morrow!"

How many to-morrows is she going to remain here? Oh! Impossible! Not an *hour* must be wasted. By the morning light

Margaret Wolfe Hungerford

something must be put on foot to save the girl from her own foolhardiness, nay ignorance!

Once again, sunk in the meshes of depression, the persecuted professor descends to the room where Hardinge awaits him.

"Anything new?" demands the latter, springing to his feet.

"Yes! Mrs. Mulcahy came up." The professor's face is so gloomy, that Hardinge may be forgiven for saying to himself, "She has assaulted him!"

"I'm glad it isn't visible," says he, staring at the professor's nose, and then at his eye. Both are the usual size.

"Eh?" says the professor. "She was visible of course. She was kinder than I expected."

"So, I see. She might so easily have made it your lip - or your nose - or -"

"*What* is there in Everett's cupboard besides the beer?" demands the professor angrily. "For Heaven's sake! attend to me, and don't sit there grinning like a first-class chimpanzee!"

This is extremely rude, but Hardinge takes no notice of it.

"I tell you she was kind - kinder than one would expect," says the professor, rapping his knuckles on the table.

"Oh! I see. She? Miss Wynter?"

"No - Mrs. Mulcahy!" roars the professor frantically. "Where's your head, man? Mrs. Mulcahy came into the room, and took Miss Wynter into her charge in the - er - the most wonderful way, and carried her off to bed." The professor mops his brow.

"Oh, well, *that's* all right," says Hardinge. "Sit down, old chap, and let's talk it over."

"It is *not* all right," says the professor. "It is all wrong. Here she is, and here she apparently means to stay. The poor child doesn't understand. She thinks I'm older than Methusaleh, and that she can live here with me. I can't explain it to her - you - don't think *you* could, do you, Hardinge?"

"No, I don't, indeed," says Hardinge, in a hurry. "What on earth has brought her here at all?"

"To *stay*. Haven't I told you? To stay for ever. She says" - with a groan - "she is going to settle me! To - to *brush my hair*! To - make my tea. She says I'm her guardian, and insists on living with me. She doesn't understand! Hardinge," desperately, "what *am* I to do?"

"Marry her!" suggests Hardinge, who I regret to say is choking with laughter.

"That is a *jest*!" says the professor haughtily. This unusual tone from the professor strikes surprise to the soul of Hardinge. He looks at him. But the professor's new humor is short-lived. He sinks upon a chair in a tired sort of a way, letting his arms fall over the sides of it. As a type of utter despair he is a distinguished specimen.

"Why don't you take her home again, back to the old aunt?" says Hardinge, moved by his misery.

"I can't. She tells me it would be useless, that the house is locked up, and - and besides, Hardinge, her aunt - after *this*, you know - would be -"

"Naturally," says Hardinge, after which he falls back upon his cigar. "Light your pipe," says he, "and we'll think it over." The professor lights it, and both men draw nearer to each other.

"I'm afraid she won't go back to her aunt any way," says the professor, as a beginning to the "thinking it over." He pushes his glasses up to his forehead, and finally discards them altogether, flinging them on the table near.

"If she saw you now she might understand," says Hardinge - for, indeed, the professor without his glasses loses thirty per cent. of old Time.

"She wouldn't," says the professor. "And never mind that. Come back to the question. I say she will never go back to her aunt."

He looks anxiously at Hardinge. One can see that he would part with a good deal of honest coin of the realm, if his companion would only *not* agree with him.

"It looks like it," said Hardinge, who is rather enjoying himself. "By Jove! what a thing to happen to *you*, Curzon, of all men in the world. What are you going to do, eh?"

"It isn't so much that," says the professor faintly. "It is what is *she* going to do?"

"*Next!*" supplements Hardinge. "Quite so! It would be a clever fellow who would answer that, straight off. I say, Curzon, what a pretty girl she is, though. Pretty isn't the word. Lovely, I -"

The professor gets up suddenly.

"Not that," says he, raising his hand in his gentle fashion - that has now something of haste in it. "It - I - you know what I mean, Hardinge. To discuss her - herself, I mean - and here -"

"Yes. You are right," says Hardinge slowly, with, however, an irrepressible stare at the professor. It is a prolonged stare. He is very fond of Curzon, though knowing absolutely nothing about him beyond the fact that he is eminently likeable; and it now strikes him as strange that this silent, awkward, ill-dressed, clever man should be the one to teach him how to behave himself. Who *is* Curzon? Given a better tailor, and a worse brain, he might be a reasonable-looking fellow enough, and not so old either - forty, perhaps - perhaps less. "Have you no relation to whom you could send her?" he says at length, that sudden curiosity as to who Curzon may be prompting the question. "Some old lady? An aunt, for example?"

"She doesn't seem to like aunts" says the professor, with deep dejection.

"Small blame to her," says, Hardinge, smoking vigorously. "*I've* an aunt - but 'that's another story!' Well - haven't you a cousin then? - or something?"

"I have a sister," says the professor slowly.

"Married?"

"A widow."

("Fusty old person, out somewhere in the wilds of Finchley," says Hardinge to himself. "Poor little girl - she won't fancy that either!")

"Why not send her to your sister then?" says he aloud.

"I'm not sure that she would like to have her," says the professor, with hesitation. "I confess I have been thinking it over for some days, but -"

"But perhaps the fact of your ward's being an heiress -" begins Hardinge - throwing out a suggestion as it were - but is checked by something in the professor's face.

"My sister is the Countess of Baring," says he gently.

Hardinge's first thought is that the professor has gone out of his mind, and his second that he himself has accomplished that deed. He leans across the table. Surprise has deprived him of his usual good manners.

"Lady Baring! - *your* sister!" says he.

CHAPTER IX

"Your face, my Thane, is as a book, where men
May read strange matters."

"I see no reason why she shouldn't be," says the professor
calmly - is there a faint suspicion of hauteur in his tone? "As
we are on the subject of myself, I may as well tell you that my
brother is Sir Hastings Curzon, of whom" - he turns back as if
to take up some imaginary article from the floor - "you may
have heard."

"Sir Hastings!" Mr. Hardinge leans back in his chair and gives
way to thought. This quiet, hard-working student - this man
whom he had counted as a nobody - the brother of that
disreputable Hastings Curzon! "As good as got the baronetcy,"
says he still thinking. "At the rate Sir Hastings is going he can't
possibly last for another twelvemonth, and here is this fellow
living in these dismal lodgings with twenty thousand a year
before his eyes. A lucky thing for him that the estates are so
strictly entailed. Good heavens! to think of a man with all that
almost in his grasp being *happy* in a coat that must have been
built in the Ark, and caring for nothing on earth but the
intestines of frogs and such-like abominations."

"You seem surprised again," says the professor, somewhat
satirically.

"I confess it," says Hardinge.

"I can't see why you should be."

"*I* do," says Hardinge drily. "That you," slowly, "*you* should be Sir Hastings' brother! Why -"

"No more!" interrupts the professor sharply. He lifts his hand. "Not another word. I know what you are going to say. It is one of my greatest troubles, that I always know what people are going to say when they mention him. Let him alone, Hardinge."

"Oh! *I'll* let him alone," says Hardinge, with a gesture of disgust. There is a pause.

"You know my sister, then?" says the professor presently.

"Yes. She is very charming. How is it I have never seen you there?"

"At her house?"

"At her receptions?"

"I have no taste for that sort of thing, and no time. Fashionable society bores me. I go and see Gwen, on off days and early hours, when I am sure that I shall find her alone. We are friends, you will understand, she and I; capital friends, though sometimes," with a sigh, "she - she seems to disapprove of my mode of living. But we get on very well on the whole. She is a very good girl," says the professor kindly, who always thinks of Lady Baring as a little girl in short frocks in her nursery - the nursery he had occupied with her.

To hear the beautiful, courted, haughty Lady Baring, who has the best of London at her feet, called "a good girl," so tickles Mr. Hardinge, that he leans back in his chair and bursts out laughing.

"Yes?" says the professor, as if asking for an explanation of the joke.

"Oh! nothing - nothing. Only - you are such a queer fellow!" says Hardinge, sitting up again to look at him. "You are a *rara avis*, do you know? No, of course you don't! You are one of the few people who don't know their own worth. I don't believe, Curzon, though I should live to be a thousand, that I shall ever look upon your like again."

"And so you laugh. Well, no doubt it is a pleasant reflection," says the professor dismally. "I begin to wish now I had never seen myself."

"Oh, come! cheer up," says Hardinge, "your pretty ward will be all right. If Lady Baring takes her in hand, she -"

"Ah! But will she?" says the professor. "Will she like Per - Miss Wynter?"

"Sure to," said Hardinge, with quite a touch of enthusiasm. "'To see her is to love her, and love but' -"

"That is of no consequence where anyone is concerned except Lady Baring," says the professor, with a little twist in his chair, "and my sister has not seen her as yet. And besides, that is not the only question - a greater one remains."

"By Jove! you don't say so! What?" demands Mr. Hardinge, growing earnest.

"Will Miss Wynter like *her*?" says the professor. "That is the real point."

"Oh! I see!" says Hardinge thoughtfully.

The next day, however, proves the professor's fears vain in both quarters. An early visit to Lady Baring, and an anxious appeal, brings out all that delightful woman's best qualities. One stipulation alone she makes, that she may see the young heiress before finally committing herself to chaperone her safely through the remainder of the season.

The professor, filled with hope, hies back to his rooms, calls for Mrs. Mulcahy, tells her he is going to take his ward for a drive, and gives that worthy and now intensely interested landlady full directions to see that Miss Wynter looks - "er - nice! you know, Mrs. Mulcahy, her *best* suit, and -"

Mrs. Mulcahy came generously to the rescue.

"Her best frock, sir, I suppose, an' her Sunday bonnet. I've often wished it before, Mr. Curzon, an' I'm thinkin' that 'twill be the makin' of ye; an' a handsome, purty little crathur she is an' no mistake. An' who is to give away the poor dear, sir, askin' yer pardon?"

"I am," says the professor.

"Oh no, sir; the likes was never known. 'Tis the the father or one of his belongings as gives away the bride, *niver* the husband to be, 'an if ye *have* nobody, sir, you two, why I'm sure I'd be proud to act for ye in this matther. Faix I don't disguise from ye, Misther Curzon, dear, that I feels like a mother to that purty child this moment, an' I tell ye *this*, that if ye don't behave dacent to her, ye'll have to answer to Mrs. Mulcahy for that same."

"What d'ye mean, woman?" roars the professor, indignantly. "Do you imagine that I -?"

"No. I'd belave nothin' bad o' ye," says Mrs. Mulcahy solemnly. "I've cared ye these six years, an' niver a fault to find. But that child beyant, whin ye take her away to make her yer wife -"

"You must be mad," says the professor, a strange, curious pang contracting his heart. "I am not taking her away to - I - I am taking her to my sister, who will receive her as a guest."

"Mad!" repeats Mrs. Mulcahy furiously. "Who's mad? Faix," preparing to leave the room, "'tis yerself was born widout a grain o' sinse!"

The meeting between Lady Baring and Perpetua is eminently satisfactory. The latter, looking lovely, but a little frightened, so takes Lady Baring's artistic soul by storm, that that great lady then and there accepts the situation, and asks Perpetua if she will come to her for a week or so. Perpetua, charmed in turn by Lady Baring's grace and beauty and pretty ways, receives the invitation with pleasure, little dreaming that she is there "on view," as it were, and that the invitation is to be prolonged indefinitely - that is, till either she or her hostess tire one of the other.

The professor's heart sinks a little as he sees his sister rise and loosen the laces round the girl's pretty, slender throat, begging her to begin to feel at home at once. Alas! He has deliberately given up his ward! *His* ward! Is she any longer his? Has not the great world claimed her now, and presently will she not belong to it? So lovely, so sweet she is, will not all men run to snatch the prize? - a prize, bejewelled too, not only by Nature, but by that gross material charm that men call wealth. Well, well, he has done his best for her. There was, indeed, nothing else left to do.

CHAPTER X

"The sun is all about the world we see,
The breath and strength of very Spring; and we
Live, love, and feed on our own hearts."

The lights are burning low in the conservatory, soft perfumes from the many flowers fill the air. From beyond - somewhere - (there is a delicious drowsy uncertainty about the where) - comes the sound of music, soft, rhymical, and sweet. Perhaps it is from one of the rooms outside - dimly seen through the green foliage - where the lights are more brilliant, and forms are moving. But just in here there is no music save the tinkling drip, drip of the little fountain that plays idly amongst the ferns.

Lady Baring is at home to-night, and in the big, bare rooms outside dancing is going on, and in the smaller rooms, tiny tragedies and comedies are being enacted by amateurs, who, oh, wondrous tale! do know their parts and speak them, albeit no stage "proper" has been prepared for them. Perhaps that is why stage-fright is not for them - a stage as big as "all the world" leaves actors very free.

But in here - here, with the dainty flowers and dripping fountains, there is surely no thought of comedy or tragedy. Only a little girl gowned all in white, with snowy arms and neck, and diamonds gittering in the soft masses of her waving hair. A happy little girl, to judge by the soft smile upon her

Margaret Wolfe Hungerford

lovely lips, and the gleam in her dark eyes. Leaning back in her seat in the dim, cool recesses of the conservatory, amongst the flowers and the greeneries, she looks like a little nymph in love with the silence and the sense of rest that the hour holds.

It is broken, however.

"I am so sorry you are not dancing," says her companion, leaning towards her. His regret is evidently genuine, indeed, to Hardinge the evening is an ill-spent one that precludes his dancing with Perpetua Wynter.

"Yes?" she looks up at him from her low lounge amongst the palms. "Well, so am I, do you know!" telling the truth openly, yet with an evident sense of shame. "But I don't dance now because - it is selfish, isn't it? - because I should be so unhappy afterwards if I *did*!"

"A perfect reason," says Hardinge very earnestly. He is still leaning towards her, his elbows on his knees, his eyes on hers. It is an intent gaze that seldom wanders, and in truth why should it? Where is any other thing as good to look at as this small, fair creature, with the eyes, and the hair, and the lips that belong to her?

He has taken possession of her fan, and gently, lovingly, as though indeed it is part of her, is holding it, raising it sometimes to sweep the feathers of it across his lips.

"Do you think so?" says she, as if a little puzzled. "Well, I confess I don't like the moments when I hate myself. We all hate ourselves sometimes, don't we?" looking at him as if doubtfully, "or is it only I myself, who -"

"Oh, no!" says Hardinge. "*All!* All of us detest ourselves now and again, or at least we think we do. It comes to the same thing, but you - you have no cause."

"I should have if I danced," says she, "and I couldn't bear the after reproach, so I don't do it."

"And yet - yet you would *like* to dance?"

"I don't know -" She hesitates, and suddenly looks up at him with eyes as full of sorrow as of mirth. "At all events I know *this*," says she, "that I wish the band would not play such nice waltzes!"

Hardinge gives way to laughter, and presently she laughs too, but softly, and as if afraid of being heard, and as if too a little ashamed of herself. Her color rises, a delicate warm color that renders her absolutely adorable.

"Shall I order them to stop?" asks Hardinge, laughing still, yet with something in his gaze that tells her he *would* forbid them to play if he could, if only to humor her.

"No!" says she, "and after all," - philosophically - "enjoyment is only a name."

"That's all!" says Hardinge, smiling. "But a very good one."

"Let us forget it," with a little sigh, "and talk of something else, something pleasanter."

"Than enjoyment?"

She gives way to his mood and laughs afresh.

"Ah! you have me there!" says she.

"I have not, indeed," he returns, quietly and with meaning. "Neither there, nor anywhere."

He gets up suddenly, and going to her, bends over the chair on which she is sitting.

"We were talking of what?" asks she, with admirable courage, "of names, was it not? An endless subject. *My* name now? An absurd one surely. Perpetua! I don't like Perpetua, do you?" She is evidently talking at random.

"I do indeed!" says Hardinge, promptly and fervently. His tone accentuates his meaning.

"Oh, but so harsh, so unusual!"

"Unusual! That in itself constitutes a charm."

"I was going to add, however - disagreeable."

"Not that - never that," Says Hardinge.

"You mean to say you really *like* Perpetua?" her large soft eyes opening with amazement.

"It is a poor word," says he, his tone now very low. "If I dared say that I *adored* 'Perpetua,' I should be -"

"Oh, you laugh at me," interrupts she with a little impatient gesture, "you *know* how crude, how strange, how -"

"I don't indeed. Why should you malign yourself like that? You - *you* - who are - "

He stops short, driven to silence by a look in the girl's eyes.

"What have *I* to do with it? I did not christen myself," says she. There is perhaps a suspicion of hauteur in her tone. "I am talking to you about my *name*. You understand that, don't you?" - the hauteur increasing. "Do you know, of late I have often wished I was somebody else, because then I should have had a different one."

Hardinge, at this point, valiantly refrains from a threadbare quotation. Perhaps he is too far crushed to be able to remember it.

"Still it is charming," says he, somewhat confusedly.

"It is absurd," says Perpetua coldly. There is evidently no pity in her. And alas! when we think what *that* sweet feeling is akin to, on the highest authority, one's hopes for Hardinge fall low. He loses his head a little.

"Not so absurd as your guardian's, however," says he, feeling the necessity for saying something without the power to manufacture it.

"Mr. Curzon's? What is his name?" asks she, rising out of her lounging position and looking, for the first time, interested.

"Thaddeus."

Perpetua, after a prolonged stare, laughs a little.

"What a name!" says she. "Worse than mine. And yet," still laughing, "it suits him, I think."

Hardinge laughs with her. Not *at* his friend, but *with* her. It seems clear to him that Perpetua is making gentle fun of her guardian, and though his conscience smites him for encouraging her in her naughtiness, still he cannot refrain.

"He is an awfully good old fellow," says he, throwing a sop to his Cerberus.

"Is he?" says Perpetua, as if even *more* amused. She looks up at him, and then down again, and trifles with the fan she has taken back from him, and finally laughs again; something in her laugh this time, however, puzzles him.

"You don't like him?" hazards he. "After all, I suppose it is hardly natural that a ward *should* like her guardian."

"Yes? And *why*?" asks Perpetua, still smiling, still apparently amused.

"For one thing, the sense of restraint that belongs to the relations between them. A guardian, you know, would be able to control one in a measure."

"Would he?"

"Well, I imagine so. It is traditionary. And you?"

"I don't know about *other* people," says Miss Wynter, calmly, "I know only this, that nobody ever yet controlled *me*, and I don't suppose now that anybody ever will."

As she says this she looks at him with the prettiest smile; it is a mixture of amusement and defiance. Hardinge, gazing at her, draws conclusions. ("Perfectly *hates* him," decides he.)

It seems to him a shame, and a pity too, but after all, old Curzon was hardly meant by Nature to do the paternal to a strange and distinctly spoilt child, and a beauty into the bargain.

"I don't think your guardian will have a good time," says he, bending over her confidentially, on the strength of this decision of his.

"Don't you?" She draws back from him and looks up. "You think I shall lead him a very bad life?"

"Well, as *he* would regard it. Not as I should," with a sudden, impassioned glance.

Miss Wynter puts that glance behind her, and perhaps there is something - something a little dangerous in the soft, *soft* look she now turns upon him.

"He thinks so, too, of course?" says she, ever so gently. Her tone is half a question, half an assertion. It is manifestly unfair, the whole thing. Hardinge, believing in her tone, her smile, falls into the trap. Mindful of that night when the professor in despair at her untimely descent upon him, had said many things unmeant, he answers her.

"Hardly that. But -"

"Go on."

"There was a little word or two, you know," laughing.

"A hint?" laughing too, but how strangely! "Yes? And -?"

"Oh! a *mere* hint! The professor is too loyal to go beyond that. I suppose you know you have the best man in all the world for your guardian? But it was a little unkind of your people, was it not, to give you into the keeping of a confirmed bookworm - a savant - with scarcely a thought beyond his studies?"

"He could study me!" says she. "I should be a fresh specimen."

"A *rara avis*, indeed! but not such as the professor's soul covets. No, believe me, you are as dust before the wind in his learned eye."

"You think then - that I - am a trouble to him?"

"It is inconceivable," says he, with a shrug of apology, "but he has no room in his daily thoughts, I verily believe, for anything beyond his beloved books, and notes, and discoveries."

"Yet *I* am a discovery," persists she, looking at him with anxious eyes, and leaning forward, whilst her fan falls idly on her knees.

"Ah! But so unpardonably *recent*!" returns he with a smile.

"True!" says she. She gives him one swift brilliant glance, and then suddenly grows restless. "How *warm* it is!" she says fretfully. "I wish -"

What she was going to say, will never now be known. The approach of a tall, gaunt figure through the hanging oriental curtains at the end of the conservatory checks her speech. Sir Hastings Curzon is indeed taller than most men, and is, besides, a man hardly to be mistaken again when once seen. Perpetua has seen him very frequently of late.

CHAPTER XI

"But all was false and hollow; though his tongue
Dropped manna, and could make the worse appear
The better reason, to perplex and dash
Maturest counsels."

"Shall I take you to Lady Baring?" says Hardinge, quickly, rising and bending as if to offer her his arm.

"No, thank you," coldly.

"I think," anxiously, "you once told me you did not care for Sir -"

"Did I? It seems quite terrible the amount of things I have told everybody." There is a distinct flash in her lovely eyes now, and her small hand has tightened round her fan. "Sometimes - I talk folly! As a fact" (with a touch of defiance), "I like Sir Hastings, although he *is* my guardian's brother! - my guardian who would so gladly get rid of me." There is bitterness on the young, red mouth.

"You should not look at it in that light."

"Should I not? You should be the last to say that, seeing that you were the one to show me how to regard it. Besides, you forget Sir Hastings is Lady Baring's brother too, and - you haven't anything to say against *her*, have you? Ah!" with a sudden lovely smile, "you, Sir Hastings?"

"You are not dancing," says the tall, gaunt man, who has now come up to her. "So much I have seen. Too warm? Eh? You show reason, I think. And yet, if I might dare to hope that you would give me this waltz -"

"No, no," says she, still with her most charming air. "I am not dancing to-night. I shall not dance this year."

"That is a Median law, no doubt," says he. "If you will not dance with me, then may I hope that you will give me the few too short moments that this waltz may contain?"

Hardinge makes a vague movement but an impetuous one. If the girl had realized the fact of his love for her, she might have been touched and influenced by it, but as it is she feels only a sense of anger towards him. Anger unplaced, undefined, yet nevertheless intense.

"With pleasure," says she to Sir Hastings, smiling at him almost across Hardinge's outstretched hand. The latter draws back.

"You dismiss me?" says he, with a careful smile. He bows to her - he is gone.

"A well-meaning young man," says Sir Hastings, following Hardinge's retreating figure with a delightfully lenient smile. "Good-looking too; but earnest. Have you noticed it? Entirely well-bred, but just a little earnest! *Such* a mistake!"

"I don't think that," says Perpetua. "To be earnest! One *should* be earnest."

"Should one?" Sir Hastings looks delighted expectation. "Tell me about it," says he.

"There is nothing to tell," says Perpetua, a little petulantly perhaps. This tall, thin man! what a *bore* he is! And yet, the other - Mr. Hardinge - well *he* was worse; he was a *fool*, anyway; he didn't understand the professor one bit! "I like Mr. Hardinge," says she suddenly.

"Happy Hardinge! But little girls like you are good to everyone, are you not? That is what makes you so lovely. You could be good to even a scapegrace, eh? A poor, sad outcast like me?" He laughs and leans towards her, his handsome, dissipated, abominable face close to hers.

Involuntarily she recoils.

"I hope everyone is good to you," says she. "Why should they not be? And why do you call yourself an outcast? Only bad people are outcasts. And bad people," slowly, "are not known, are they?"

"Certainly not," says he, disconcerted. This little girl from a far land is proving herself too much for him. And it is not her words that disconcert him so much as the straight, clear, open glance from her thoughtful eyes.

To turn the conversation into another channel seems desirable to him.

"I hope you are happy here with my sister," says he, in his anything but everyday tone.

"Quite happy, thank you. But I should have been happier still, I think, if I had been allowed to stay with your brother."

Sir Hastings drops his glasses. Good heavens! what kind of a girl is this!

"To stay with my brother! To *stay*," stammers he.

"Yes. He *is* your brother, isn't he? The professor, I mean. I should quite have enjoyed living with him, but he wouldn't hear of it. He - he doesn't like me, I'm afraid?" Perpetua looks at him anxiously. A little hope that he will contradict Hardinge's statement animates her mind. To feel herself a burden to her guardian - to anyone - she, who in the old home had been nothing less than an idol! Surely Sir Hastings, his own brother, will say something, will tell her something to ease this chagrin at her heart.

"Who told you that?" asks Sir Hastings. "Did he himself? I shouldn't put it beyond him. He is a misogynist; a mere bookworm! Of no account. Do not waste a thought on him."

"You mean -?"

"That he detests the best part of life - that he has deliberately turned his back on all that makes our existence here worth the having. I should call him a fool, but that one so dislikes having an imbecile in one's family."

"The best part of life! You say he has turned his back on that." She lets her hands fall upon her knees, and turns a frowning, perplexed, but always lovely face to his. "What is it," asks she, "that best part?"

"Women!" returns he, slowly, undauntedly, in spite of the innocence, the serenity, that shines in the young and exquisite face before him.

Her eyes do not fall before his. She is plainly thinking. Yes; Mr. Hardinge was right, he will never like her. She is only a stay, a hindrance to him!

"I understand," says she sorrowfully. "He will not care - *ever*. I shall be always a trouble to him. He -"

"Why think of him?" says Sir Hastings contemptuously. He leans towards her: fired by her beauty, that is now enhanced by the regret that lies upon her pretty lips, he determines on pushing his cause at once. "If *he* cannot appreciate you, others can - *I* can. I -" He pauses; for the first time in his life, on such an occasion as this, he is conscious of a feeling of awkwardness. To tell a woman he loves her has been the simplest thing in the world hitherto, but now, when at last he is in earnest - when poverty has driven him to seek marriage with an heiress as a cure for all his ills - he finds himself tongue-tied; and not only by the importance of the situation, so far as money goes, but by the clear, calm, waiting eyes of Perpetua.

"Yes?" says she; and then suddenly, as if not caring for the answer she has demanded. "You mean that he - You, *too*, think that he dislikes me?" There is woe in the pale, small, lovely face.

"Very probably. He was always eccentric. Perfect nuisance at home. None of us could understand him. I shouldn't in the least wonder if he had taken a rooted aversion to you, and taken it badly too! Miss Wynter! It quite distresses me to think that it should be *my* brother, of all men, who has failed to see your charm. A charm that -" He pauses effectively, to let his really fine eyes have some play. The conservatory is sufficiently dark to disguise the ravages that dissipation has made upon his handsome features. He can see that Perpetua is regarding him earnestly, and with evident interest. Already he regards his cause as won. It is plain that the girl is attracted by his face, as indeed she is! She is at this moment asking herself, who is it he is like?

"You were saying?" says she dreamily.

"That the charm you possess, though of no value in the eyes of your guardian, is, to *me*, indescribably attractive. In fact - I -"

A second pause, meant to be even more effective.

Perpetua turns her gaze more directly upon him. It occurs to her that he is singularly dull, poor man.

"Go on," says she. She nods her head at him with much encouragement.

Her encouragement falls short. Sir Hastings, who had looked for girlish confusion, is somewhat disconcerted by this open patronage.

"May I?" says he - "You *permit* me then to tell you what I have so longed, feared to disclose. I" - dramatically - "*love you!*"

He is standing over her, his hand on the back of her chair, waiting for the swift blush, the tremor, the usual signs that follow on one of his declarations. Alas! there is no blush now, no tremor, no sign at all.

"That is very good of you," says Perpetua, in an even tone. She moves a little away from him, but otherwise shows no emotion whatever. "The more so, in that it must be so difficult for you to love a person in fourteen days! Ah! that is kind, indeed."

A curious light comes into Sir Hastings' eyes. This little Australian girl, is she *laughing* at him? But the fact is that Perpetua is hardly thinking of him at all, or merely as a shadow to her thoughts. Who *is* he like? that is the burden of her inward song. At this moment she knows. She lifts her head to see the professor standing in the curtained doorway down below. Ah! yes, that is it! And, indeed, the resemblance between the two brothers is wonderfully strong at this instant! In the eyes of both a quick fire is kindled.

CHAPTER XII

"Love, like a June rose,
Buds and sweetly blows -
But tears its leaves disclose,
And among thorns it grows."

The professor had been standing inside the curtain for a full minute before Perpetua had seen him. Spell-bound he had stood there, gazing at the girl as if bewitched. Up to this he had seen her only in black - black always - severe, cold - but *now*!

It is to him as though he had seen her for the first time. The graceful curves of her neck, her snowy arms, the dead white of the gown against the whiter glory of the soft bosom, the large, dark eyes so full of feeling, the little dainty head! Are they *all* new - or some sweet, fresher memory of a picture well beloved?

Then he had seen his brother! - Hastings - the disgrace, the *roue* ... and bending over *her*!... There had been that little movement, and the girl's calm drawing back, and -

The professor's step forward at that moment had betrayed him to Perpetua.

She rises now, letting her fan fall without thought to the ground.

Margaret Wolfe Hungerford

"You!" cries she, in a little, soft, quick way. "*You!*" Indeed it seems to her impossible that it can be he.

She almost runs to him. If she had quite understood Sir Hastings is impossible to know, for no one has ever asked her since, but certainly the advent of her guardian is a relief to her.

"You!" she says again, as if only half believing. Her gaze grows bewildered. If he had never seen her in anything but black before, she had never seen him in ought but rather antiquated morning clothes. Is this really the professor? Her eyes ask the question anxiously. This tall, aristocratic, perfectly-appointed man; this man who looks positively *young*. Where are the glasses that until now hid his eyes? Where is that old, old coat?

"Yes." Yes, the professor certainly and as disagreeable as possible. His eyes are still aflame; but Perpetua is not afraid of him. She is angry with him, in a measure, but not afraid. One *might* be afraid of Sir Hastings, but of Mr. Curzon, no!

The professor had seen the glad rush of the girl towards him, and a terrible pang of delight had run through all his veins - to be followed by a reaction. She had come to him because she *wanted* him, because he might be of use to her, not because.... What had Hastings been saying to her? His wrathful eyes are on his brother rather than on her when he says:

"You are tired?"

"Yes," says Perpetua.

"Shall I take you to Gwendoline?"

"Yes," says Perpetua again.

"Miss Wynter is in my care at present," says Sir Hastings, coming indolently forward. "Shall I take you to Lady Baring?" asks he, addressing Perpetua with a suave smile.

"She will come with me," says the professor, with cold decision.

"A command!" says Sir Hastings, laughing lightly. "See what it is, Miss Wynter, to have a hard-hearted guardian." He shrugs his shoulders. Perpetua makes him a little bow, and follows the professor out of the conservatory.

"If you are tired," says the professor, somewhat curtly, and without looking at her, "I should think the best thing you could do would be to go to bed!"

This astounding advice receives but little favor at Miss Wynter's hands.

"I am tired of your brother," says she promptly. "He is as tiresome a creation as I know - but not of your sister's party; and - I'm too old to be sent to bed, even by a *Guardian*!!" She puts a very big capital to the last word.

"I don't want to send you to bed," says the professor simply. "Though I think little girls like you -"

"I am not a little girl," indignantly.

"Certainly you are not a big one," says he. It is an untimely remark. Miss Wynter's hitherto ill-subdued anger now bursts into flame.

"I can't help it if I'm not big," cries she. "It isn't my fault. I can't help it either that papa sent me to you. *I* didn't want to go to you. It wasn't my fault that I was thrown upon your hands. And - and" - her voice begins to tremble - "it isn't my fault either that you *hate* me."

"That I - hate you!" The professor's voice is cold and shocked.

"Yes. It is true. You need not deny it. You *know* you hate me." They are now in an angle of the hall where few people come and go, and are, for the moment, virtually alone.

"Who told you that I hated you?" asks the professor in a peremptory sort of way.

"No," says she, shaking her head, "I shall not tell you that, but I have heard it all the same."

"One hears a great many things if one is foolish enough to listen," Curzon's face is a little pale now. "And - I can guess who has been talking to you."

"Why should I not listen? It is true, is it not?"

She looks up at him. She seems tremulously anxious for the answer.

"You want me to deny it then?"

"Oh, no, *no!*" she throws out one hand with a little gesture of mingled anger and regret. "Do you think I want you to *lie* to me? There I am wrong. After all," with a half smile, sadder than most sad smiles because of the youth and sweetness of it, "I do not blame you. I *am* a trouble, I suppose, and all troubles are hateful. I" - holding out her hand - "shall take your advice, I think, and go to bed."

"It was bad advice," says Curzon, taking the hand and holding it. "Stay up, enjoy yourself, dance -"

"Oh! I am not dancing," says she as if offended.

"Why not?" eagerly, "Better dance than sleep at your age. You - you mistook me. Why go so soon?"

She looks at him with a little whimsical expression.

"I shall not know you *at all*, presently," says she. "Your very appearance to-night is strange to me, and now your sentiments! No, I shall not be swayed by you. Good-night, good-bye!" She smiles at him in the same sorrowful little way, and takes a step or two forward.

"Perpetua," says the professor sternly, "before you go you must listen to me. You said just now you would not hear me lie to you - you shall hear only the truth. Whoever told you that I hated you is the most unmitigated liar on record!"

Perpetua rubs her fan up and down against her cheek for a little bit.

"Well - I'm glad you don't hate me," says she, "but still I'm a worry. Never mind," - sighing - "I daresay I shan't be so for long."

"You mean?" asks the professor anxiously.

"Nothing - nothing at all. Good-night. Good-night, *indeed*."

"Must you go? Is enjoyment nothing to you?"

"Ah! you have killed all that for me," says she. This parting shaft she hurls at him - *malice prepense*. It is effectual. By it she murders sleep as thoroughly as ever did Macbeth. The professor spends the remainder of the night pacing up and down his rooms.

CHAPTER XIII

"Through thick and thin, both over bank and bush,
In hopes her to attain by hook or crook.

"You will begin to think me a fixture," says Hardinge with a somewhat embarrassed laugh, flinging himself into an armchair.

"You know you are always welcome," says the professor gently, if somewhat absently.

It is next morning, and he looks decidedly the worse for his sleeplessness. His face seems really old, his eyes are sunk in his head. The breakfast lying untouched upon the table tells its own tale.

"Dissipation doesn't agree with you," says Hardinge with a faint smile.

"No. I shall give it up," returns Curzon, his laugh a trifle grim.

"I was never more surprised in my life than when I saw you at your sister's last evening. I was relieved, too - sometimes it is necessary for a man to go out, and - and see how things are going on with his own eyes."

"I wonder when that would be?" asks the professor indifferently.

"When a man is a guardian," replies Hardinge promptly, and with evident meaning.

The professor glances quickly at him.

"You mean -?" says he.

"Oh! yes, of course I mean something," says Hardinge impatiently. "But I don't suppose you want me to explain myself. You were there last night - you must have seen for yourself."

"Seen what?"

"Pshaw!" says Hardinge, throwing up his head, and flinging his cigarette into the empty fireplace. "I saw you go into the conservatory. You found her there, and - *him*. It is beginning to be the chief topic of conversation amongst his friends just now. The betting is already pretty free."

"Go on," says the professor.

"I needn't go on. You know it now, if you didn't before."

"It is you who know it - not I. *Say it!*" says the professor, almost fiercely. "It is about her?"

"Your ward? Yes. Your brother it seems has made his mind to bestow upon her his hand, his few remaining acres, and," with a sneer, "his spotless reputation."

"*Hardinge!*" cries the professor, springing to his feet as if shot. He is evidently violently agitated. His companion mistakes the nature of his excitement.

"Forgive me!" says he quickly. "Of course *nothing* can excuse my speaking of him like that - to you. But I feel you ought to be told. Miss Wynter is in your care, you are in a measure responsible for her future happiness - the happiness of her whole *life*, Curzon - and if anything goes wrong with her -"

The professor puts up his hand as if to check him. He has grown ashen-grey, and the other hand resting on the back of the chair is visibly trembling.

"Nothing shall go wrong with her," says he, in a curious tone.

Hardinge regards him keenly. Is this pallor, this unmistakable trepidation, caused only by his dislike to hear his brother's real character exposed.

"Well, I have told you," says he coldly.

"It is a mistake," says the professor. "He would not dare to approach a young, innocent girl. The most honorable proposal such a man as he could make to her would be basely dishonorable."

"Ah! you see it in that light too," says Hardinge, with a touch of relief. "My dear fellow, it is hard for me to discuss him with you, but yet I fear it must be done. Did you notice nothing in his manner last night?"

Yes, the professor *had* noticed something. Now there comes back to him that tall figure stooping over Perpetua, the handsome, leering face bent low - the girl's instinctive withdrawal.

"Something must be done," says he.

"Yes. And quickly. Young girls are sometimes dazzled by men of his sort. And Per - Miss Wynter ... Look here, Curzon," breaking off hurriedly. "This is *your* affair, you know. You are her guardian. You should see to it."

"I could speak to her."

"That would be fatal. She is just the sort of girl to say 'Yes' to him because she was told to say 'No.'"

"You seem to have studied her," says the professor quietly.

"Well, I confess I have seen a good deal of her of late."

"And to some purpose. Your knowledge of her should lead you to making a way out of this difficulty."

"I have thought of one," says Hardinge boldly, yet with a quick flush. "You are her guardian. Why not arrange another marriage for her, before this affair with Sir Hastings goes too far."

"There are two parties to a marriage," says the professor, his tone always very low. "Who is it to whom you propose to marry Miss Wynter?"

Hardinge, getting up, moves abruptly to the window and back again.

"You have known me a long time, Curzon," says he at last. "You - you have been my friend. I have family - position - money - I -"

"I am to understand, then, that *you* are a candidate for the hand of my ward," says the professor slowly, so slowly that it might suggest itself to a disinterested listener that he has great difficulty in speaking at all.

"Yes," says Hardinge, very diffidently. He looks appealingly at the professor. "I know perfectly well she might do a great deal better," says he, with a modesty that sits very charmingly upon him. "But if it comes to a choice between me and your brother, I - I think I am the better man. By Jove, Curzon," growing hot, "it's awfully rude of me, I know, but it is so hard to remember that he *is* your brother."

But the professor does not seem offended. He seems, indeed,

so entirely unimpressed by Hardinge's last remark, that it may reasonably be supposed he hasn't heard a word of it.

"And she?" says he. "Perpetua. Does she -" He hesitates as if finding it impossible to go on.

"Oh! I don't know," says the younger man, with a rather rueful smile. "Sometimes I think she doesn't care for me more than she does for the veriest stranger amongst her acquaintances, and sometimes -" expressive pause.

"Yes? Sometimes?"

"She has seemed kind."

"Kind? How kind?"

"Well - friendly. More friendly than she is to others. Last night she let me sit out three waltzes with her, and, she only sat out one with your brother."

"Is it?" asks the professor, in a dull, monotonous sort of way. "Is it - I am not much in your or her world, you know - is it a very marked thing for a girl to sit out three waltzes with one man?"

"Oh, no. Nothing very special. I have known girls do it often, but she is not like other girls, is she?"

The professor waves this question aside.

"Keep to the point," says he.

"Well, *she* is the point, isn't she? And look here, Curzon, why aren't you of our world? It is your own fault surely; when one sees your sister, your brother, and - and *this*," with a slight glance round the dull little apartment, "one cannot help wondering why you -"

"Let that go by," says the professor. "I have explained it before. I deliberately chose my own way in life, and I want nothing more than I have. You think, then, that last night Miss Wynter gave you - encouragement?"

"Oh! hardly that. And yet - she certainly seemed to like - that is not to *dislike* my being with her: and once - well," - confusedly - "that was nothing."

"It must have been something."

"No, really; and I shouldn't have mentioned it either - not for a moment."

The professor's face changes. The apathy that has lain upon it for the past five minutes now gives way to a touch of fierce despair. He turns aside, as if to hide the tell-tale features, and going to the window, gazes sightlessly on the hot, sunny street below.

What was it - *what?* Shall he ever have the courage to find out? And is this to be the end of it all? In a flash the coming of the girl is present before him, and now, here is her going. Had she - had she - what *was* it he meant? No wonder if her girlish fancy had fixed itself on this tall, handsome, young man, with his kindly, merry ways and honest meaning. Ah! that was what she meant perhaps when last night she had told him "she would not be a worry to him *long*." Yes, she had meant that; that she was going to marry Hardinge!

But to *know* what Hardinge means! A torturing vision of a little lovely figure, gowned all in white - of a little lovely face uplifted - of another face down bent! No! a thousand times, no! Hardinge would not speak of that - it would be too sacred; and yet this awful doubt -

"Look here. I'll tell you," says Hardinge's voice at this moment. "After all, you are her guardian - her father almost - though I know you scarcely relish your position; and you ought to know about it, and perhaps you can give me your opinion, too, as to whether there was anything in it, you know. The fact is, I," - rather shamefacedly - "asked her for a flower out of her bouquet, and she gave it. That was all, and," hurriedly, "I don't really believe she meant anything *by* giving it, only," with a nervous laugh, "I keep hoping she *did*!"

A long, long sigh comes through the professor's lips straight from his heart. Only a flower she gave him! Well -

"What do *you* think?" asks Hardinge after a long pause.

"It is a matter on which I could not think."

"But there is this," says Hardinge. "You will forward my cause rather than your brother's, will you not? This is an extraordinary demand to make I know - but - I also know *you*."

"I would rather see her dead than married to my brother," says the professor, slowly, distinctly.

"And -?" questions Hardinge.

The professor hesitates a moment, and then:

"What do you want me to do?" asks he.

"Do? 'Say a good word for me' to her; that is the old way of putting it, isn't it? and it expresses all I mean. She reveres you, even if -"

"If what?"

"She revolts from your power over her. She is high-spirited, you know," says Hardinge. "That is one of her charms, in my opinion. What I want you to do, Curzon, is to - to see her at once - not to-day, she is going to an afternoon at Lady Swanley's - but to-morrow, and to - you know," - nervously -

"to make a formal proposal to her."

The professor throws back his head and laughs aloud. Such a strange laugh.

"I am to propose to her - I?" says he.

"For me, of course. It is very usual," says Hardinge. "And you are her guardian, you know, and -"

"Why not propose to her yourself?" says the professor, turning violently upon him. "Why give me this terrible task? Are you a coward, that you shrink from learning your fate except at the hands of another - another who -"

"To tell you the truth, that is it," interrupts Hardinge, simply. "I don't wonder at your indignation, but the fact is, I love her so much, that I fear to put it to the touch myself. You *will* help me, won't you? You see, you stand in the place of her father, Curzon. If you were her father, I should be saying to you just what I am saying now."

"True," says the professor. His head is lowered. "There, go," says he, "I must think this over."

"But I may depend upon you" - anxiously - "you will do what you can for me?"

"I shall do what I can for *her*."

Margaret Wolfe Hungerford

CHAPTER XIV

"Now, by a two-headed Janus,
Nature hath framed strange fellows in her time."

Hardinge is hardly gone before another - a far heavier - step sounds in the passage outside the professor's door. It is followed by a knock, almost insolent in its loudness and sharpness.

"What a hole you do live in," says Sir Hastings, stepping into the room, and picking his way through the books and furniture as if afraid of being tainted by them. "Bless me! what strange beings you scientists are. Rags and bones your surroundings, instead of good flesh and blood. Well, Thaddeus - hardly expected to see *me* here, eh?"

"You want me?" says the professor. "Don't sit down there - those notes are loose; sit here."

"Faith, you've guessed it, my dear fellow, I *do* want you, and most confoundedly badly this time. Your ward, now, Miss Wynter! Deuced pretty little girl, isn't she, and good form too? Wonderfully bred - considering."

"I don't suppose you have come here to talk about Miss Wynter's good manners."

"By Jove! I have though. You see, Thaddeus, I've about come

to the length of my tether, and - er - I'm thinking of turning over a new leaf - reforming, you know - settling down - going in for dulness - domesticity, and all the other deuced lot of it."

"It is an excellent resolution, that might have been arrived at years ago with greater merit," says the professor.

"A preacher and a scientist in one! Dear sir, you go beyond the possible," says Sir Hastings, with a shrug. "But to business. See here, Thaddeus. I have told you a little of my plans, now hear the rest. I intend to marry - an heiress, *bien entendu* - and it seems to me that your ward, Miss Wynter, will suit me well enough."

"And Miss Wynter, will you suit *her* well enough?"

"A deuced sight too well, I should say. Why, the girl is of no family to signify, whereas the Curzons - It will be a better match for her than in her wildest dreams she could have hoped for."

"Perhaps, in her wildest dreams, she hoped for a good man, and one who could honestly love her."

"Pouf! You are hardly up to date, my dear fellow. Girls, now-a-days, are wise enough to know they can't have everything, and she will get a good deal. Title, position - I say, Thaddeus, what I want of you i to - er - to help me in this matter - to - crack me up a bit, eh? - to - *you* know."

The professor is silent, more through disgust than want of anything to say. Staring at the man before him, he knows he is loathsome to him - loathsome, and his own brother! This man, who with some of the best blood of England in his veins, is so far, far below the standard that marks the gentleman. Surely vice is degrading in more ways than one. To the professor, Sir Hastings, with his handsome, dissipated face, stands out, tawdry, hideous, vulgar - why, every word he says is tinged with coarseness; and yet, what a pretty boy he used to be, with his soft, sunny hair and laughing eyes -

"You will help me, eh?" persists Sir Hastings, with his little dry chronic cough, that seems to shake his whole frame.

"Impossible," says the professor, simply, coldly.

"*No?* Why?"

The professor looks at him (a penetrating glance), but says nothing.

"Oh! damn it all!" says his brother, his brow darkening. "You had *better*, you know, if you want the old name kept above water much longer."

"You mean -?" says the professor, turning a grave face to his.

"Nothing but what is honorable. I tell you I mean to turn over a new leaf. 'Pon my soul, I mean *that*. I'm sick of all this old racket, it's killing me. And my title is as good a one as she can find anywhere, and if I'm dipped - rather - her money would pull me straight again, and -"

He pauses, struck by something in the professor's face.

"You mean -?" says the latter again, even more slowly. His eyes are beginning to light.

"Exactly what I have said," sullenly. "You have heard me."

"Yes, I *have* heard you," cries the professor, flinging aside all restraints and giving way to sudden violent passion - the more violent, coming from one so usually calm and indifferent. "You have come here to-day to try and get possession, not only of the fortune of a young and innocent girl, but of her body and *soul* as well! And it is me, *me* whom you ask to be a party to this shameful transaction. Her dead father left her to my care, and I am to sell her to you, that her money may redeem our name from the slough into which *you* have flung it? Is innocence to be sacrificed that vice may ride abroad again? Look here," says the professor, his face deadly white, "you have come to the wrong man. I shall warn Miss Wynter against marriage with *you*, as long as there is breath left in my body."

Sir Hastings has risen too; *his* face is dark red; the crimson flood has reached his forehead and dyed it almost black. Now, at this terrible moment, the likeness between the two brothers, so different in spirit, can be seen; the flashing-eyes, the scornful lips, the deadly hatred. It is a shocking likeness, yet not to be denied.

"What do *you* mean, damn you?" says Sir Hastings; he sways a little, as if his passion is overpowering him, and clutches feebly at the edge of the table.

"Exactly what *I* have said," retorts the professor, fiercely.

"You refuse then to go with me in this matter?"

"*Finally.* Even if I would, I could not. I - have other views for her."

"Indeed! Perhaps those other views include yourself. Are you thinking of reserving the prize for your own special benefit? A penniless guardian - a rich ward; as a situation, it is perfect; full of possibilities."

"Take care," says the professor, advancing a step or two.

"Tut! Do you think I can't see through your game?" says Sir Hastings, in his most offensive way, which is nasty indeed. "You hope to keep me unmarried. You tell yourself, I can't live much longer, at the pace I'm going. I know the old jargon - I have it by heart - given a year at the most the title and the heiress will both be yours! I can read you - I -" He breaks off to laugh sardonically, and the cough catching him, shakes him horribly. "But, no, by heaven!" cries he. "I'll destroy your hopes yet. I'll disappoint you. I'll marry. I'm a young man yet - yet - with life - *long* life before me - life -"

A terrible change comes over his face, he reels backwards, only saving himself by a blind clinging to a book-case on his right.

The professor rushes to him and places his arm round him. With his foot he drags a chair nearer, into which Sir Hastings falls with a heavy groan. It is only a momentary attack, however; in a little while the leaden hue clears away, and, though still ghastly, his face looks more natural.

"Brandy," gasps he faintly. The professor holds it to his lips, and after a minute or two he revives sufficiently to be able to sit up and look round him.

"Thought you had got rid of me for good and all," says he, with a malicious grin, terrible to see on his white, drawn face. "But I'll beat you yet! There! - Call my fellow - he's below. Can't get about without a damned attendant in the morning, now. But I'll cure all that. I'll see you dead before I go to my own grave. I -"

"Take your master to his carriage," says the professor to the man, who is now on the threshold. The maunderings of Sir Hastings - still hardly recovered from his late fit - strike horribly upon his ear, rendering him almost faint.

CHAPTER XV

My love is like the sky,
As distant and as high;
Perchance she's fair and kind and bright,
Perchance she's stormy - tearful quite -
Alas! I scarce know why."

It is late in the day when the professor enters Lady Baring's house. He had determined not to wait till the morrow to see Perpetua. It seemed to him that it would be impossible to go through another sleepless night, with this raging doubt, this cruel uncertainty in his heart.

He finds her in the library, the soft light of the dying evening falling on her little slender figure. She is sitting in a big armchair, all in black - as he best knows her - with a book upon her knee. She looks charming, and fresh as a new-born flower. Evidently neither last night's party nor to-day's afternoon have had power to dim her beauty. Sleep had visited *her* last night, at all events.

She springs out of her chair, and throws her book on the table near her.

"Why, you are the very last person I expected," says she.

"No doubt," says the professor. Who was the *first* person she has expected? And will Hardinge be here presently to plead his

Margaret Wolfe Hungerford

cause in person? "But it was imperative I should come. There is something I have to tell you - to lay before you."

"Not a mummy, I trust," says she, a little flippantly.

"A proposal," says the professor, coldly. "Much as I know you dislike the idea, still; it was your poor father's wish that I should, in a measure, regulate your life until your coming of age. I am here to-day to let you know - that - Mr. Hardinge has requested me to tell you that he -"

The professor pauses, feeling that he is failing miserably. He, the fluent speaker at lectures, and on public platforms, is now bereft of the power to explain one small situation.

"What's the matter with Mr. Hardinge," asks Perpetua, "that he can't come here himself? Nothing serious, I hope?"

"I am your guardian," says the professor - unfortunately, with all the air of one profoundly sorry for the fact declared, "and he wishes *me* to tell you that he - is desirous of marrying you."

Perpetua stares at him. Whatever bitter thoughts are in her mind, she conceals them.

"He is a most thoughtful young man," says she, blandly. "And - and you're another."

"I hope I am thoughtful, if I am not young," says the professor, with dignity. Her manner puzzles him. "With regard to Hardinge, I wish you to know that - that I - have known him for years, and that he is in my opinion a strictly honorable, kind-hearted man. He is of good family. He has money. He will probably succeed to a baronetcy - though this is not *certain*, as his uncle is, comparatively speaking, young still. But, even without the title, Hardinge is a man worthy of any woman's esteem, and confidence, and -"

He is interrupted by Miss Wynter's giving way to a sudden

burst of mirth. It is mirth of the very angriest, but it checks him the more effectually, because of that.

"You must place great confidence in princes!" says she. "Even '*without* the title, he is worthy of esteem.'" She copies him audaciously. "What has a title got to do with esteem? - and what has esteem got to do with love?"

"I should hope -" begins the professor.

"You needn't. It has nothing to do with it, nothing *at all.* Go back and tell Mr. Hardinge so; and tell him, too, that when next he goes a-wooing, he had better do it in person."

"I am afraid I have damaged my mission," says the professor, who has never once looked at her since his first swift glance.

"*Your* mission?"

"Yes. It was mere nervousness that prevented him coming to you first himself. He said he had little to go on, and he said something about a flower that you gave him -"

Perpetua makes a rapid movement toward a side table, takes a flower from a bouquet there, and throws it at the professor. There is no excuse to be made for her beyond the fact that her heart feels breaking, and people with broken hearts do strange things every day.

"I would give a flower to *anyone!*" says she in a quick scornful fashion. The professor catches the ungraciously given gift, toys with it, and - keeps it. Is that small action of his unseen?

"I hope," he says in a dull way, "that you are not angry with him because he came first to me. It was a sense of duty - I know, I *feel* - compelled him to do it, together with his honest diffidence about your affection for him. Do not let pride stand in the way of -"

"Nonsense!" says Perpetua, with a rapid movement of her hand. "Pride has no part in it. I do not care for Mr. Hardinge - I shall not marry him."

A little mist seems to gather before the professor's eyes. His glasses seem in the way, he drops them, and now stands gazing at her as if disbelieving his senses. In fact he does disbelieve in them.

"Are you sure?" persists he. "Afterwards you may regret -"

"Oh, no!" says she, shaking her head. "*Mr. Hardinge* will not be the one to cause me regret."

"Still think -"

"Think! Do you imagine I have not been thinking?" cries she, with sudden passion. "Do you imagine I do not know why you plead his cause so eloquently? You want to get *rid* of me. You are *tired* of me. You always thought me heartless, about my poor father even, and unloving, and - hateful, and -"

"Not heartless; what have I done, Perpetua, that you should say that?"

"Nothing. That is what I *detest* about you. If you said outright what you were thinking of me, I could bear it better."

"But my thoughts of you. They are -" He pauses. What *are* they? What are his thoughts of her at all hours, all seasons? "They are always kind," says he, lamely, in a low tone, looking at the carpet. That downward glance condemns him in her eyes - to her it is but a token of his guilt towards her.

"They are *not*!" says she, with a little stamp of her foot that makes the professor jump. "You think of me as a cruel, wicked, worldly girl, who would marry *anyone* to gain position."

Here her fury dies away. It is overcome by something stronger.

She trembles, pales, and finally bursts into a passion of tears that have no anger in them, only an intense grief.

"I do not," says the professor, who is trembling too, but whose utterance is firm. "Whatever my thoughts are, *your* reading of them is entirely wrong."

"Well, at all events you can't deny one thing," says she checking her sobs, and gazing at him again with undying enmity. "You want to get rid of me, you are determined to marry me to some one, so as to get me out of your way. But I shan't marry to please *you*. I needn't either. There is somebody else who wants to marry me besides your - *your* candidate!" with an indignant glance. "I have had a letter from Sir Hastings this afternoon. And," rebelliously, "I haven't answered it yet."

"Then you shall answer it now," says the professor. "And you shall say 'no' to him."

"Why? Because you order me?"

"Partly because of that. Partly because I trust to your own instincts to see the wisdom of so doing."

"Ah! you beg the question," says she, "but I'm not so sure I shall obey you for all that."

"Perpetua! Do not speak to me like that, I implore you," says the professor, very pale. "Do you think I am not saying all this for your good? Sir Hastings - he is my brother - it is hard for me to explain myself, but he will not make you happy."

"Happy! *You* think of my happiness?"

"Of what else?" A strange yearning look comes into his eyes. "God knows it is *all* I think of," says he.

"And so you would marry me to Mr. Hardinge?"

"Hardinge is a good man, and he loves you."

"If so, he is the only one on earth who does," cries the girl bitterly. She turns abruptly away, and struggles with herself for a moment, then looks back at him. "Well. I shall not marry him," says she.

"That is in your own hands," says the professor. "But I shall have something to say about the other proposal you speak of."

"Do you think I want to marry your brother?" says she. "I tell you no, no, *no*! A thousand times no! The very fact that he *is* your brother would prevent me. To be your ward is bad enough, to be your sister-in-law would be insufferable. For all the world I would not be more to you than I am now."

"It is a wise decision," says the professor icily. He feels smitten to his very heart's core. Had he ever dreamed of a nearer, dearer tie between them? - if so the dream is broken now.

"Decision?" stammers she.

"Not to marry my brother."

"Not to be more to you, you mean!"

"You don't know what you are saying," says the professor, driven beyond his self-control. "You are a mere child, a baby, you speak at random."

"What!" cries she, flashing round at him, "will you deny that I have been a trouble to you, that you would have been thankful had you never heard my name?"

"You are right," gravely. "I deny nothing. I wish with all my soul I had never heard your name. I confess you troubled me. I go beyond even *that*, I declare that you have been my undoing! And now, let us make an end of it. I am a poor man and a busy one, this task your father laid upon my shoulders is too heavy for me. I shall resign my guardianship; Gwendoline - Lady Baring - will accept the position. She likes you, and - you will find it hard to break *her* heart."

"Do you mean," says the girl, "that I have broken yours? *Yours?* Have I been so bad as that? Yours? I have been wilful, I know, and troublesome, but troublesome people do not break one's heart. What have I done then that yours should be broken?" She has moved closer to him. Her eyes are gazing with passionate question into his.

"Do not think of that," says the professor, unsteadily. "Do not let that trouble you. As I just now told you, I am a poor man, and poor men cannot afford such luxuries as hearts."

"Yet poor men have them," says the girl in a little low stifled tone. "And - and girls have them too!"

There is a long, long silence. To Curzon it seems as if the whole world has undergone a strange, wild upheaval. What had she meant - what? Her words! Her words meant something, but her looks, her eyes, oh, how much more *they* meant! And yet to listen to her - to believe - he, her guardian, a poor man, and she an heiress! Oh! no. Impossible.

"So much the worse for the poor men," says he deliberately.

There is no mistaking his meaning. Perpetua makes a little rapid movement towards him - an almost imperceptible one. *Did* she raise her hands as if to hold them out to him? If so, it is so slight a gesture as scarcely to be remembered afterwards, and at all events the professor takes no notice of it, presumably, therefore, he does not see it.

"It is late," says Perpetua a moment afterwards. "I must go and dress for dinner." *Her* eyes are down now. She looks pale and shamed.

"You have nothing to say, then?" asks the professor,

compelling himself to the question.

"About what?"

"Hardinge."

The girl turns a white face to his.

"Will you then *compel* me to marry him?" says she. "Am I" - faintly - "nothing to you? Nothing -" She seems to fade back from him in the growing uncertainty of the light into the shadow of the corner beyond. Curzon makes a step towards her.

At this moment the door is thrown suddenly open, and a man - evidently a professional man - advances into the room.

"Sir Thaddeus," begins he, in a slow, measured way.

The professor stops dead short. Even Perpetua looks amazed.

"I regret to be the messenger of bad news, sir," says the solemn man in black. "They told me I should find you here. I have to tell you, Sir Thaddeus, that your brother, the late lamented Sir Hastings is dead." The solemn man spread his hands abroad.

CHAPTER XVI

'Till the secret be secret no more
In the light of one hour as it flies,
Be the hour as of suns that expire
  Or suns that rise."

It is quite a month later. August, hot and sunny, is reigning with quite a mad merriment, making the most of the days that be, knowing full well that the end of the summer is nigh. The air is stifling; up from the warm earth comes the almost overpowering perfume of the late flowers. Perpetua moving amongst the carnations and hollyhocks in her soft white cambric frock, gathers a few of the former in a languid manner to place in the bosom of her frock. There they rest, a spot of blood color upon their white ground.

Lady Baring, on the death of her elder brother, had left town for the seclusion of her country home, carrying Perpetua with her. She had grown very fond of the girl, and the fancy she had formed (before Sir Hastings' death) that Thaddeus was in love with the young heiress, and that she would make him a suitable wife, had not suffered in any way through the fact of Sir Thaddeus having now become the head of the family.

Perpetua, having idly plucked a few last pansies, looked at them, and as idly flung them away, goes on her listless way through the gardens. A whole *long* month and not one word from him! Are his social duties now so numerous that he has forgotten he has a ward? "Well," emphatically, and with a vicious little tug at her big white hat, "*some* people have strange views about duty."

She has almost reached the summer-house, vine-clad, and temptingly cool in all this heat, when a quick step behind her causes her to turn.

"They told me you were here," says the professor, coming up with her. He is so distinctly the professor still, in spite of his new mourning, and the better cut of his clothes, and the general air of having been severely looked after - that Perpetua feels at home with him at once.

"I have been here for some time," says she calmly. "A whole month, isn't it?"

"Yes, I know. Were you going into that green little place. It looks cool."

It is cool, and particularly empty. One small seat occupies the back of it, and nothing else at all, except the professor and his ward.

"Perpetua!" says he, turning to her. His tone is low, impassioned. "I have come. I could not come sooner, and I *would* not write. How could I put it all on paper? You remember that last evening?"

"I remember," says she faintly.

"And all you said?"

"All *you* said."

"I said nothing. I did not dare. *Then* I was too poor a man, too insignificant to dare to lay bare to you the thoughts, the fears, the hopes that were killing me."

"Nothing!" echoes she. "Have you then forgotten?" She raises her head, and casts at him a swift, but burning glance. "*Was* it nothing? You came to plead your friend's cause, I think. Surely that was something? I thought it a great deal. And what was it you said of Mr. Hardinge? Ah! I *have* forgotten that, but I know how you extolled him - praised him to the skies - recommended him to me as a desirable suitor." She makes an impatient movement, as if to shake something from her. "Why have you come to-day?" asks she. "To plead his cause afresh?"

"Not his - to-day."

"Whose then? Another suitor, maybe? It seems I have more than even I dreamt of."

"I do not know if you have dreamed of this one," says Curzon, perplexed by her manner. Some hope had been in his heart in his journey to her, but now it dies. There is little love truly in her small, vivid face, her gleaming eyes, her parted, scornful lips.

"I am not given to dreams," says she, with a petulant shrug, "*I* know what I mean always. And as I tell you, if you *have* come here to-day to lay before me, for my consideration, the name of another of your friends who wishes to marry me, why I beg you to save yourself the trouble. Even the country does not save me from suitors. I can make my choice from many, and when I *do* want to marry, I shall choose for myself."

"Still - if you would permit me to name *this* one," begins Curzon, very humbly, "it can do you no harm to hear of him. And it all lies in your own power. You can, if you will, say yes, or -" He pauses. The pause is eloquent, and full of deep entreaty.

"Or no," supplies she calmly. "True! You," with a half defiant, half saucy glance, "are beginning to learn that a guardian cannot control one altogether."

"I don't think I ever controlled you, Perpetua."

"N - o! Perhaps not. But then you tried to. That's worse."

"Do you forbid me then to lay before you - this name - that I -?"

"I have told you," says she, "that I can find a name for myself."

"You forbid me to speak," says he slowly.

"*I* forbid! A ward forbid her guardian! I should be afraid!" says she, with an extremely naughty little glance at him.

"You trifle with me," says the professor slowly, a little sternly, and with uncontrolled despair. "I thought - I believed - I was *mad* enough to imagine, from your manner to me that last night we met, that I was something more than a mere guardian to you."

"More than *that*. That seems to be a Herculean relation. What more would you be?"

"I am no longer that, at all events."

"What!" cries she, flushing deeply. "You - you give me up -"

"It is you who give *me* up."

"You say you will no longer be my guardian!" She seems struck with amazement at this declaration on his part. She had not believed him when he had before spoken of his intention of resigning. "But you cannot," says she. "You have promised. Papa *said* you were to take care of me."

"Your father did not know."

"He *did*. He said you were the one man in all the world he could trust."

"Impossible," says the professor. "A - lover - cannot be a guardian!" His voice has sunk to a whisper. He turns away, and makes a step towards the door.

"You are going," cries she, fighting with a desperate desire for tears, that is still strongly allied to anger. "You would leave me. You will be no longer my guardian, Ah! was I not right? Did I not *tell* you you were in a hurry to get rid of me?"

This most unfair accusation rouses the professor to extreme wrath. He turns round and faces her like an enraged lion.

"You are a child," says he, in a tone sufficient to make any woman resentful. "It is folly to argue with you."

"A child! What are you then?" cries she tremulously.

"A *fool!*" furiously. "I was given my cue, I would not take it. You told me that it was bad enough to be your ward, that you would not on any account be closer to me. *That* should have been clear to me, yet, like an idiot, I hoped against hope. I took false courage from each smile of yours, each glance, each word. There! Once I leave you now, the chain between us will be broken, we shall never, with *my* will, meet again. You say you have had suitors since you came down here. You hinted to me that you could mention the name of him you wished to marry. So be it. Mention it to Gwendoline - to any one you like, but not to me."

He strides towards the doorway. He has almost turned the corner.

"Thaddeus" cries a small, but frantic voice. If dying he would hear that and turn. She is holding out her hands to him, the tears are running down her lovely cheeks.

"It is to you - to *you* I would tell his name," sobs she, as he returns slowly, unwillingly, but *surely*, to her. "To you alone."

"To me! Go on," says Curzon; "let me hear it. What is the name of this man you want to marry?"

"Thaddeus Curzon!" says she, covering her face with her hands, and, indeed, it is only when she feels his arms round her, and his heart beating against hers, that she so far recovers herself as to be able to add, "And a *hideous* name it is, too!"

But this last little firework does no harm. Curzon is too ecstatically happy to take notice of her small impertinence.

Choose from Thousands of 1stWorldLibrary Classics By

A. M. Barnard
Ada Leverson
Adolphus William Ward
Aesop
Agatha Christie
Alexander Aaronsohn
Alexander Kielland
Alexandre Dumas
Alfred Gatty
Alfred Ollivant
Alice Duer Miller
Alice Turner Curtis
Alice Dunbar
Allen Chapman
Ambrose Bierce
Amelia E. Barr
Amory H. Bradford
Andrew Lang
Andrew McFarland Davis
Andy Adams
Anna Alice Chapin
Anna Sewell
Annie Besant
Annie Hamilton Donnell
Annie Payson Call
Annie Roe Carr
Annonaymous
Anton Chekhov
Arnold Bennett
Arthur Conan Doyle
Arthur M. Winfield
Arthur Ransome
Arthur Schnitzler
Atticus
B.H. Baden-Powell
B. M. Bower
B. C. Chatterjee
Baroness Emmuska Orczy
Baroness Orczy
Basil King
Bayard Taylor
Ben Macomber
Bertha Muzzy Bower
Bjornstjerne Bjornson
Booth Tarkington
Boyd Cable
Bram Stoker
C. Collodi
C. E. Orr

C. M. Ingleby
Carolyn Wells
Catherine Parr Traill
Charles A. Eastman
Charles Amory Beach
Charles Dickens
Charles Dudley Warner
Charles Farrar Browne
Charles Ives
Charles Kingsley
Charles Klein
Charles Hanson Towne
Charles Lathrop Pack
Charles Romyn Dake
Charles Whibley
Charles Willing Beale
Charlotte M. Braeme
Charlotte M. Yonge
Charlotte Perkins Stetson
Clair W. Hayes
Clarence Day Jr.
Clarence E. Mulford
Clemence Housman
Confucius
Coningsby Dawson
Cornelis DeWitt Wilcox
Cyril Burleigh
D. H. Lawrence
Daniel Defoe
David Garnett
Dinah Craik
Don Carlos Janes
Donald Keyhoe
Dorothy Kilner
Dougan Clark
Douglas Fairbanks
E. Nesbit
E.P.Roe
E. Phillips Oppenheim
Earl Barnes
Edgar Rice Burroughs
Edith Van Dyne
Edith Wharton
Edward Everett Hale
Edward J. O'Biren
Edward S. Ellis
Edwin L. Arnold
Eleanor Atkins
Eliot Gregory

Elizabeth Gaskell
Elizabeth McCracken
Elizabeth Von Arnim
Ellem Key
Emerson Hough
Emilie F. Carlen
Emily Dickinson
Enid Bagnold
Enilor Macartney Lane
Erasmus W. Jones
Ernie Howard Pie
Ethel May Dell
Ethel Turner
Ethel Watts Mumford
Eugenie Foa
Eugene Wood
Eustace Hale Ball
Evelyn Everett-green
Everard Cotes
F. H. Cheley
F. J. Cross
F. Marion Crawford
Federick Austin Ogg
Ferdinand Ossendowski
Francis Bacon
Francis Darwin
Frances Hodgson Burnett
Frances Parkinson Keyes
Frank Gee Patchin
Frank Harris
Frank Jewett Mather
Frank L. Packard
Frank V. Webster
Frederic Stewart Isham
Frederick Trevor Hill
Frederick Winslow Taylor
Friedrich Kerst
Friedrich Nietzsche
Fyodor Dostoyevsky
G.A. Henty
G.K. Chesterton
Gabrielle E. Jackson
Garrett P. Serviss
Gaston Leroux
George A. Warren
George Ade
Geroge Bernard Shaw
George Durston
George Ebers

George Eliot
George Gissing
George MacDonald
George Meredith
George Orwell
George Sylvester Viereck
George Tucker
George W. Cable
George Wharton James
Gertrude Atherton
Gordon Casserly
Grace E. King
Grace Gallatin
Grace Greenwood
Grant Allen
Guillermo A. Sherwell
Gulielma Zollinger
Gustav Flaubert
H. A. Cody
H. B. Irving
H.C. Bailey
H. G. Wells
H. H. Munro
H. Irving Hancock
H. Rider Haggard
H. W. C. Davis
Haldeman Julius
Hall Caine
Hamilton Wright Mabie
Hans Christian Andersen
Harold Avery
Harold McGrath
Harriet Beecher Stowe
Harry Castlemon
Harry Coghill
Harry Houidini
Hayden Carruth
Helent Hunt Jackson
Helen Nicolay
Hendrik Conscience
Hendy David Thoreau
Henri Barbusse
Henrik Ibsen
Henry Adams
Henry Ford
Henry Frost
Henry James
Henry Jones Ford
Henry Seton Merriman
Henry W Longfellow
Herbert A. Giles

Herbert Carter
Herbert N. Casson
Herman Hesse
Hildegard G. Frey
Homer
Honore De Balzac
Horace B. Day
Horace Walpole
Horatio Alger Jr.
Howard Pyle
Howard R. Garis
Hugh Lofting
Hugh Walpole
Humphry Ward
Ian Maclaren
Inez Haynes Gillmore
Irving Bacheller
Isabel Hornibrook
Israel Abrahams
Ivan Turgenev
J.G.Austin
J. Henri Fabre
J. M. Barrie
J. Macdonald Oxley
J. S. Fletcher
J. S. Knowles
J. Storer Clouston
Jack London
Jacob Abbott
James Allen
James Andrews
James Baldwin
James Branch Cabell
James DeMille
James Joyce
James Lane Allen
James Lane Allen
James Oliver Curwood
James Oppenheim
James Otis
James R. Driscoll
Jane Austen
Jane L. Stewart
Janet Aldridge
Jens Peter Jacobsen
Jerome K. Jerome
John Burroughs
John Cournos
John F. Kennedy
John Gay
John Glasworthy

John Habberton
John Joy Bell
John Kendrick Bangs
John Milton
John Philip Sousa
Jonas Lauritz Idemil Lie
Jonathan Swift
Joseph A. Altsheler
Joseph Carey
Joseph Conrad
Joseph E. Badger Jr
Joseph Hergesheimer
Joseph Jacobs
Jules Vernes
Julian Hawthrone
Julie A Lippmann
Justin Huntly McCarthy
Kakuzo Okakura
Kenneth Grahame
Kenneth McGaffey
Kate Langley Bosher
Kate Langley Bosher
Katherine Cecil Thurston
Katherine Stokes
L. A. Abbot
L. T. Meade
L. Frank Baum
Latta Griswold
Laura Dent Crane
Laura Lee Hope
Laurence Housman
Lawrence Beasley
Leo Tolstoy
Leonid Andreyev
Lewis Carroll
Lewis Sperry Chafer
Lilian Bell
Lloyd Osbourne
Louis Hughes
Louis Tracy
Louisa May Alcott
Lucy Fitch Perkins
Lucy Maud Montgomery
Luther Benson
Lydia Miller Middleton
Lyndon Orr
M. Corvus
M. H. Adams
Margaret E. Sangster
Margret Howth
Margaret Vandercook

Margret Penrose
Maria Edgeworth
Maria Thompson Daviess
Mariano Azuela
Marion Polk Angellotti
Mark Overton
Mark Twain
Mary Austin
Mary Catherine Crowley
Mary Cole
Mary Hastings Bradley
Mary Roberts Rinehart
Mary Rowlandson
M. Wollstonecraft Shelley
Maud Lindsay
Max Beerbohm
Myra Kelly
Nathaniel Hawthrone
Nicolo Machiavelli
O. F. Walton
Oscar Wilde
Owen Johnson
P.G. Wodehouse
Paul and Mabel Thorne
Paul G. Tomlinson
Paul Severing
Percy Brebner
Peter B. Kyne
Plato
R. Derby Holmes
R. L. Stevenson
R. S. Ball
Rabindranath Tagore
Rahul Alvares
Ralph Bonehill
Ralph Henry Barbour
Ralph Victor
Ralph Waldo Emmerson
Rene Descartes
Rex Beach

Rex E. Beach
Richard Harding Davis
Richard Jefferies
Richard Le Gallienne
Robert Barr
Robert Frost
Robert Gordon Anderson
Robert L. Drake
Robert Lansing
Robert Lynd
Robert Michael Ballantyne
Robert W. Chambers
Rosa Nouchette Carey
Rudyard Kipling
Samuel B. Allison
Samuel Hopkins Adams
Sarah Bernhardt
Sarah C. Hallowell
Selma Lagerlof
Sherwood Anderson
Sigmund Freud
Standish O'Grady
Stanley Weyman
Stella Benson
Stella M. Francis
Stephen Crane
Stewart Edward White
Stijn Streuvels
Swami Abhedananda
Swami Parmananda
T. S. Ackland
T. S. Arthur
The Princess Der Ling
Thomas A. Janvier
Thomas A Kempis
Thomas Anderton
Thomas Bailey Aldrich
Thomas Bulfinch
Thomas De Quincey
Thomas Dixon

Thomas H. Huxley
Thomas Hardy
Thomas More
Thornton W. Burgess
U. S. Grant
Valentine Williams
Various Authors
Vaughan Kester
Victor Appleton
Victoria Cross
Virginia Woolf
Wadsworth Camp
Walter Camp
Walter Scott
Washington Irving
Wilbur Lawton
Wilkie Collins
Willa Cather
Willard F. Baker
William Dean Howells
William le Queux
W. Makepeace Thackeray
William W. Walter
William Shakespeare
Winston Churchill
Yei Theodora Ozaki
Yogi Ramacharaka
Young E. Allison
Zane Grey

www.ingramcontent.com/pod-product-compliance
Lightning Source LLC
Chambersburg PA
CBHW030755150426
42813CB00068B/3136/J